LEAVING FAITH BEHIND

*Paul,
Best wishes
Keep on singing*

Ralph Olsen

Paul,
Best wishes
Keep on Singing
Jeff Obrow

LEAVING FAITH BEHIND

Jeffrey Olsson

Copyright © 2009 by Jeffrey Olsson.

ISBN:	Hardcover	978-1-4415-0681-8
	Softcover	978-1-4415-0680-1

All rights reserved. No part of this book may be reproduced or transmitted in any form or by any means, electronic or mechanical, including photocopying, recording, or by any information storage and retrieval system, without permission in writing from the copyright owner.

This book was printed in the United States of America.

To order additional copies of this book, contact:
Xlibris Corporation
1-888-795-4274
www.Xlibris.com
Orders@Xlibris.com
58554

Table of Contents

(1) A Letter to My Curious Friends 7
(2) Realization 10
(3) Residential Schools 12
(4) Treatment of Homosexuals 16
(5) Living Waters 18
(6) Stripping My Faith Bare 20
(7) What Do I Believe 22
(8) Morality 25
(9) End of A letter to My Curious Friends 27
(10) Watching TV 29
(11) Atheoi 32
(12) Atheism Is More Than a Word 35
(13) How do I know? 37
(14) Authority 40
(15) Tenacity, Faith and Authority 42
(16) Rationalism 47
(17) Empiricism 49
(18) Flashes of Light—finding our inner bias 52
(19) Bumps in the night—Animism 58
(20) Morality Evolved 63
(21) Moral Equipment 67
(22) St. Augustine's Morality 73
(23) Disappointment 76
(24) The Encyclopedias 79
(25) A Brief Glimpse at Evolution 82
(25) Anglicanism and Homosexuality 89
(26) Honest Doubt 98
(27) Hope 101

Appendix 1—Further explanation of the concept "taught not to question" 111
Appendix 2—The problem with inerrant holy books 115
Appendix 3—Table: Quick Reference—Ways of knowing 118
References 121

(1)

A Letter to My Curious Friends

Many of you have asked why I would want to leave a faith community such as the Anglican Church of Canada. The truth of the matter is that I had contemplated leaving long in advance of actually doing so. The intention of this letter is simply to explain why I left. This is my personal story, and the message I tell in this story is deeply meaningful to me.

Some people, even some of my friends, have started to make up their own reasons as to why I left the Church, none of which are based on any sort of fact. My intention in writing this letter is to explain my personal reasons. This is not to attack the Christian faith; however, I will be frank and honest, as I had good reason to leave the church behind. I will also present a rationale that explains why it is so important that I do not return to Christianity. If you have trouble with this type of thinking, and I know some of you will, I suggest that you do not read this letter. Put it down.

Before I left the church I spoke with my closest friends and explained the troubles I was having with what I saw going on. I thought very carefully about how to reconcile my differences of opinion but I could not see how to bridge the gap. When I was finally in a position to see the system of belief adhered to by people within the church as the root of the problem, it didn't take me very long to see what I had to do. So I left.

In my letter of resignation I stated it to my Bishop like this

"I have given many hours of thought to my role within the Anglican Church of Canada. I have considered and reconsidered whether I should return to St. Aidan's or if I should carry on as a priest at all. During my time off I have identified three issues at the centre of my discomfort with the Anglican Communion. The first is my own faith in God. The second is the same sex [marriage] issue. The third is the manner in which the leadership of this institution handles conflict, including the residential schools issue. Since these issues are not easily separated, I will explain in detail."

Faith in God seems like a no-brainer to many people, but not for me. In fact, it has not always been easy for me to call myself a Christian. Perhaps this explains why I sought out increasing amounts of education and responsibility within the church. As I look back, I see that I did this to create for myself a "Christian Reality". I also did this, in part, because it made an easy fit with my family and friends. Please believe me when I say that this reasoning fits well with the motivations I have felt. In years past, I spent many evenings and weekends, preparing sermons, counseling, teaching in classrooms and studying. As time went on, I began to feel quite competent about my abilities. I felt I could explain things well. My ability to believe increased with this competence. However, during my quiet times I still wondered if a loving God was a reality, especially in the world that we live in, including what happened in the residential schools.

I became a Christian when I was only a child, at 12 years of age. I encouraged my father and mother to come to church and ultimately this lead to their involvement in the Christian community. When I first became a Christian it was because I sincerely believed it when I was told that God loves me. A few years later, when I reconsidered my decision for logical reasons, one of my close friends reminded me about why I should be afraid to leave.

"It's an incredible price to pay", he said, "eternal damnation, there is no end to it and yet the solution is so simple, all we have to do is believe and trust in God, it's so simple"

At the time the risk seemed too great, I cowered and retreated. I stopped questioning the validity of my faith. I lived in a remote northern town and I had no more information to go on than that offered by the Christian community.

Please don't misunderstand me, I knew people who were atheistic, but they offered no real arguments to me. Had they offered an argument that was stronger than the wonderful feelings of security and comfort offered to me by the church I would have reconsidered my faith again. I carried on in the church as a happy and enthusiastic member, and considered God to be a reality that was a challenge to be understood. I viewed seeking God as a worthwhile endeavor.

(2)

Realization

> "I have never seen the slightest scientific proof of the religious theories of heaven and hell, of future life for individuals, or of a personal God."
> —Thomas Edison (1847-1931), in Columbian magazine

In my late 20's I attended diocesan ministry training to prepare for the priesthood and I was ordained and appointed rector of my own small parish in northern Manitoba when I was 32. 5 years later when I had moved to Winnipeg I was appointed to the position of honorary assistant to the rector of another parish in the diocese of Rupertsland, I felt my spiritual world slowly begin to crumble.

In Winnipeg I faced criticism from other clergy on petty matters, some of the parishioners jumped in to help criticize. I no longer felt competent. I remember one communion service where, I was almost paralyzed, afraid to make a mistake in procedure because the rector was so particular. I had seen him openly criticize others in front of large groups of people, and I did not want that to happen to me.

It was not long before I began to question the validity of my calling again. Was I really meant for this ministry? At first I questioned my own calling and competence but later on I began to question the existence of a personal God. As I watched the news I wondered, "How can such awful things happen in a world where a loving God is present?". Why won't God intervene?

As I began to question God's existence I felt the need to question the validity of scripture and the identity of Jesus Christ. Did Jesus really perform miracles? Or was Jesus like one of today's charlatan ministers who prey on people's credulity? Images of Benny Hinn's TV ministry flashed through my mind. Is this really as good as it gets?

Without a real God who works as creator and maintainer of this world everything else is up in the air. Christian faith is revealed as a wishful creation of humankind. Could it be that Christianity is nothing more than a cultural phenomenon?

An ancient Philosopher named Epicurus (BC 341-270) summed up my problem in this manner:

"Is God willing to prevent evil, but not able? Then he is not omnipotent.

Is he able, but not willing? Then he is malevolent.

Is he both able and willing? Then where does evil come from?

Is he neither able nor willing? Then why call him God?"

(3)

Residential Schools

"Sunday School: A prison in which children do penance for the evil conscience of their parents."—H.L. Mencken (1880-1956), editor and critic, in A Menken Chrestomathy

While I worked up north I was painfully aware of the residential schools issue in which aboriginal children were taken from their homes and sent off to be scrubbed and shorn, educated and converted to the ways of mainstream "Christian" society of the 1800's-1960's. I worked with a number of families affected by this program, counseling them as a priest would. It often amazed me that they attended church at all. Our church had a file with pictures of students from our area that had been sent to schools as far away as Prince Albert Saskatchewan, or Dauphin Manitoba. Both schools were approximately 800 kilometers away from where the children's families lived at the time. In some cases they were sent against the parents wishes, as Canadian law demanded this schooling for aboriginal students.

I found myself deeply moved by their stories of abuse and prayed with them; I asked God to help them find healing and peace. As I heard their testimony it created deep conflicts within me. How could a loving God allow this to happen, especially at the hands of Christians? Since I was much younger than any of the residential school victims in Gillam I did not appear to offer the same threat as some of the older clergy did. I openly admitted the churches fault for failing to protect them from abuse. I was also open to new ways of thinking and presented God as a loving and compassionate spirit who understood what it was like to suffer. Some of those who were abused seemed to accept my testimony.

By the time I had moved to Winnipeg the lawsuits against the Canadian Government and the Anglican Church of Canada had formally begun. I witnessed, first hand, the reaction of the southern clergy as we were forced to institute restitution. At one of our diocesan meetings where over a hundred clergy and senior laity met an on annual basis, a small number of the clergy openly questioned whether or not the church was actually at fault for its role in the residential schools program. One priest described the church as a scapegoat for the Government run program. A few others stated that they did not feel any responsibility for what had happened at all.

Others discussed and developed strategies to protect the assets of the diocese, and they considered how to limit the churches responsibility in this matter. Some of these strategies were voted on and remain a part of the official church record of those meetings.

At one of these meetings a church elder took the microphone, she tried to convince a few of these people that the abuse was real and that it could have been stopped, she started to tell a story about how her own children had been abused by an Anglican priest. Some of the clergy and other elders who had earlier made a motion to protect the assets of the church made loud groans, causing her to stop speaking.

After a long silence where the woman stood crying, I looked over at the Bishop. He was staring at his shoes. Not knowing what else to do I stood up, in the midst of those listening and said "I would love to hear what you have to say". I urged her to continue telling her story. After a few moments and a few more tears she told the rest of her story and made the point that the church needs to accept responsibility, much to the chagrin of those who opposed her testimony.

Out in the parking lot after the meeting where this brave lady had challenged the ethics of those who presented the "church saving" strategies, one of the presenters came to the window of my car and asked why I was so "arrogant". He said, "You seemed so damned sure of yourself".

I wonder if he had ever met a single person who had suffered abuse through the residential school program!

Later that evening, in the privacy of prayer I wept as I faced his challenge. I felt compelled to ask the following questions:

> Is it an act of abuse to remove children from their parents, send them away to school, cut their hair off, and forbid them to speak their native tongue?
>
> Is it an act of abuse to scrub the skin of an aboriginal child with a brush, repeatedly, in an attempt to make it whiter?
>
> Is it and act of mental abuse to tell a child that they had better believe in your God or they are going to go to hell?

How is it possible to think, for even a moment, that the church is not responsible for its role in destroying the lives of some of the people in the residential schools program?

What amazes me is how students came out of these schools with any real education at all.

In his official capacity, the Bishop of our diocese apologized in a very sincere and genuine manner. I believe him. But I will never forget the words of those clergy members who so callously rejected our churches responsibility.

Quick facts about the residential school system in Canada:

150,000 children were affected by this system, which removed children from aboriginal homes and required them to attend one of 132 residential schools, which were often located in communities far from where the parents lived.

In a Globe and Mail article it was reported that a study by the chief medical officer found that "*24 Percent* of the students had died from tuberculosis over a 14 year period" at certain residential schools.

80,000 surviving students have been compensated and a formal apology by Canadian Prime Minister Stephen Harper was made in front of a sitting house of Commons.

The schools *operated from the late 1800's* until the last school closed in 1996.

RCMP fact sheets state that *Widespread social problems* have been attributed to the abuse that children suffered in these schools, including substance abuse, violence, suicide, sexual abuse, mental health issues and isolation.

http://www.informify.com/top-stories/47-law-civil-rights/222-canada-apologizes-compensates-native-people

http://www.globeadvisor.com/servlet/ArticleNews/story/gam/20070424/SCHOOLS24

http://www.cbc.ca/canada/story/2008/05/16/f-timeline-residential-schools.html

http://www.rcmp-grc.gc.ca/fs-fd/irs-spi-eng.htm

(4)

Treatment of Homosexuals

"What we call rational grounds for our beliefs are often extremely irrational attempts to justify our instincts."—Thomas Henry Huxley (1825-1895) (from Phantoms In The Brain by V.S. Ramachandran)

There is currently a national debate on the validity of homosexual practice for members of clergy of the Anglican Church of Canada. As it stands, clergy who have a homosexual orientation are not allowed to pursue a relationship. While they are allowed to practice as a priest, they must remain celibate. Anglican homosexual parishioners are not allowed to marry.

With regard to my own faith in God, the problem was that the same sex debate has one leg firmly planted in science. As I made my personal judgments on the validity of same sex relationships I consulted many sources. I first looked into the Bible and Christian books written on the subject and then I listened to those from within the scientific community. I listened carefully to those from within the Gay community as they presented their case on the radio and television. I purchased and read a number of articles and periodicals on this issue. Finally, I met with some personal friends from within the Gay community and asked them some very bold questions about how they know they are Gay. I have not taken this issue lightly!

Where the Bible clearly states that homosexuality is an abomination to God, naturalistic observation shows that it is a perfectly natural but small part of life for many mammalian species, including humankind. There is a lot of research that shows that homosexual behaviour is a commonly occurring behaviour that never "takes over" any of the populations observed.

A cursory study of basic biology will show you that even if homosexuality might be transmitted through genetic code, it will never present a serious threat to the abundance of heterosexual relationships since the homosexual act cannot result in offspring. In other words there is no gene transfer mechanism by which homosexual preference in relationships could ever "take over" as the predominant sexual behaviour in society. While the issue of homosexuality is a complicated one from a genetic viewpoint, it is clearly impossible for homosexual sex to compete with heterosexual reproduction.

There is, in fact, no "war" on the family. Or, the war would be over if conservative Christians would just look at the facts.

Even still, there are conservative Anglicans who maintain that God will remove his blessings from our country and put a curse on Canada now that the changes to marriage law have occurred.

It is important to note that this concept does not hold up from a biblical perspective any more than it does from an economic or scientific perspective. In scripture, God asked for "just a few righteous men" in order to put off the destruction of Sodom and Gomorrah. There seems to be no shortage of "righteous" believers in Canada.

The Bible says sexual preference matters where science says it does not. The Gay community says "We were born this way" while some Christians say it's a "sinful choice you have made for emotional and sexual comfort".

Some conservative Christians go as far as to say that "it will bring a curse from God on our nation". If Canada is to suffer any sort of curse, we should look to matters of foreign, internal economic and environmental policy as a source of concern. It is unacceptable to make a scapegoat out of the homosexual community.

(5)

Living Waters

"Where is my faith? Even deep down . . . there is nothing but emptiness and darkness. . . . If there be God—please forgive me. When I try to raise my thoughts to Heaven, there is such convicting emptiness that those very thoughts return like sharp knives and hurt my very soul . . . How painful is this unknown pain—I have no Faith. Repulsed, empty, no faith, no love, no zeal, . . . What do I labor for? If there be no God, there can be no soul. If there be no soul then, Jesus, You also are not true"—Mother Teresa, Letters. Teresa, Mother (2007). Mother Teresa: Come Be My Light, New York: Doubleday.

In the midst the same sex blessings debate I was asked to provide pastoral care to individuals within a small group, run by a non-clergy member of one of the local parishes. Before I understood much about homosexuality, I was placed in a position where I had heard the confessions of people who struggled with their sexuality on a daily basis. Some of these people felt same sex attraction and felt guilty about it because they wanted to draw close to God. They were told they had to forgo sex for the sake of their souls! Furthermore, there were no distinctions made between safe sex and dangerous or promiscuous sex. It was an "all or nothing" affair. I still cannot figure out how forgiving the sins of three, four, or more generations from a client's past can relieve same sex attraction. (Exodus 20:5, Deuteronomy 5:9, Exodus 34:6-7, 1 Corinthians 15:22)

I was made to feel very uncomfortable by the leader of the group who tried to justify certain Biblical statements and turn them into practical sexual advice. I became confused. Eventually, I declined my pastoral responsibility to this group because I felt guilty when asked if I could offer biblical interpretations and assistance on this matter. I could not justify these biblical statements without feeling as if I had lied about the truth.

Faced with an explosive issue on which it appears that the Bible is incorrect, I was forced to choose. Having been pressed to decide on the issue of sexuality by the church, I have landed squarely on the side of science, compassion and reason.

I can't imagine being forced to extinguish my own sexual desire for my wife in order to placate a loving God. How then, can I ever expect some one else to extinguish their own desire for their lover, homosexual or not, just to satisfy my own ideas about righteous behaviour?

Once the dominos started to fall, I realized that dogmatism was the problem.

My faith quietly subsided.

When it was over, I had found wonderful new allies in the world of science and rational thinking.

As I began to face myself I was forced to admit that for many years prior to this I had been selfishly pursuing a dogmatic agenda in which it was not proper to question the roots of the bible based decision making process.

I saw for the first time that when groups of Christians follow along dogmatically it breeds generations of people who have been taught not to question biblical authority, not to think about what they are being told. In some of the worst cases they accept bigotry without question. It is intellectually contemptible to continue this practice.

If you have a hard time accepting this idea, ask yourself about how many Anglican churches have stood up to defend the rights of homosexuals, to let them marry. How many in Winnipeg? When did you see the congregation make this effort? How many in rural Manitoba? How many in northern Manitoba? I can count the churches on two fingers.

Even the most liberal of our churches breed people who are taught not to question many of the critical issues important to life! While the most liberal churches still carry the potential to promote bigotry of various forms, the conservative church is clearly much worse.

(6)

Stripping My Faith Bare

"I would, like any other scientist, willingly change my mind if the evidence led me to do so. So I care about what's true, I care about evidence, I care about evidence as the reason for knowing what is true."—Richard Dawkins, in a BBC interview, April, 2004.

It is one thing to rebel against the abuses of my former church and another thing to deny the existence of a Christian God. Once I was over the hump of walking out the door, I pursued education as a means to understanding the world better.

Please don't misunderstand me, throughout my life I had always sought out whatever education was available to me at the time, but this time I was seeking specific education to help me understand how the world operates. I didn't want to trust an old book that I could plainly see had already gotten so many things wrong.

Over a 2 year period I had bought and read ten different books on the science of evolution, six books on the science of astronomy, seventeen books on the science and philosophy of psychology, and three books on the history of science. I devoured them! Without the simplistic viewpoint that says "God did it" I had so many questions that needed answering. I began to attend university.

I also reread the Bible. I was shocked at what I now saw written in the bible, as if I was reading it in the light of day for the first time. In my preparation for the priesthood we had training on biblical content, themes and the theology expressed in the bible. We even some training on biblical ethics, but I could not believe what I was now seeing.

I am not interested in presenting a list of mistakes from the Bible or a dissertation on God's lack of ethics in dealing with humans. Often it does nothing to convince anyone of anything and they simply see it as an attack on their faith. If you care to know, all you have to do is ask and I will share what I know, in person. See appendix 2 for further information.

Trust me, when I say I stripped my own faith bare as I reread the bible after I left the church. Much of the Bible pales when compared to the light of recent scientific discovery. I have also learned that I am able to tolerate much more ambiguity when I am not required to be dogmatic about certain things.

Through all of this I must confess I remain impressed by some of the things said by Jesus even though we now know that he didn't actually say everything attributed to him. (I failed to mention earlier that I also bought two other books, one explaining the various criticisms of the bible and another book that explains the history of the New Testament. The second book "Misquoting Jesus" explains how the New Testament has been edited over time, the evidence and how we know this to be true. It is written by Bart D. Ehrman, Chair of the department of religious studies at the University of North Carolina at Chapel Hill)

Two days before I decided to write this letter one of my closest friends asked, "So what now? Whatcha gonna do for Christmas?" My answer was a simple one, "I am going to enjoy it with my family. The idea that Saint Nick will not be popping down my chimney will not prevent me from enjoying Christmas with my family. I guess Jesus won't be there either, now that you mention it."

Throughout my life I have always remained atheistic about other religions, but never my own. I found it easy to see why I didn't want to be a Muslim, Jew, Hare Krishna, or a Mormon. What I didn't realize was that most of those same arguments could easily be applied to Christianity.

(7)

What Do I Believe

> *"I cannot believe in God when there is no scientific evidence for the existence of a supreme being and a creator."*—Jodie Foster, actress and director, in an interview in the Calgary Sun (July 10, 1997)

So what do I believe?

I do not attend any church. When I first came to realize how I felt about the topic of religion I struggled to explain my belief. I was unclear how to express my thoughts about where I stand, without seeming to go too far. How would I explain the gray areas regarding belief as opposed to unbelief?

In The God Delusion, Richard Dawkins does a brilliant job of explaining a continuum of beliefs that spans from theist to atheist. I have been greatly influenced by his writing and find that there are subtle differences that get left out of the conversation when assumptions are made about what atheists, agnostics or theists believe. By my own reckoning this continuum starts at a 1 for a devout believer and end at a 5 for a devout Christian.

1. Absolutely sure that there is a God and that he is Jesus Christ. I have a number of clergy friends who claim to "know" god exists because they have had religious experiences. I was once in this category.

2. Thinks there is a God, but knows there are some unanswered questions. Understands that others may have differing views on "who" god is but loves Jesus just the same.
3. Does not know for sure and generally understands both sides of the spectrum between belief and unbelief. Dawkins call this person an "impartial agnostic". In my experience this person often thinks that it is impossible to know for sure.
4. Thinks there is probably not a God. This is an agnostic who has strong atheistic thoughts. This person has explored both sides of the spectrum and is left dissatisfied with religious philosophy and "proofs". There seems to be no evidence for God.
5. Absolutely sure that there is no God. This person knows that there is no God in a similar manner to a person in category 1. Often this person has a 'first hand' ability to debunk religious claims and has experience in doing so.

Now that I have shown you the continuum of beliefs I can easily explain that I am a four on this scale. I am an Agnostic who leans hard towards Atheism and I am very comfortable making this statement. It fits me well.

I have searched for explanations that prove God's existence and cannot find any that satisfy, even after having tried them. And try I did! For thirty years of my life I used faith as a means of 'knowing Jesus' until eventually my faith soured because of seeing harm done in Jesus name.

Is it possible that there is a loving God? In my humble opinion, no! Not when you consider the condition of this world. Is it possible that there ever was a God? I can't see how it would be possible but of course know one can know for certain.

Are there other reasons, aside from the ones I mentioned above why I do not believe in God? Absolutely!

The more I read books about scientific research the more I was enamored by the explanations about who we are and how we got to be who we are. The explanations given by science tell us what we are (via evolution), they tell us how we operate (biology, psychology). They tell us where we are with regard to the universe and our place on earth (Cosmology). It is very important to point out that science, as we know it today, is not the final word on many issues. New hypotheses may be made, with new ways of proving and testing, theories may change. Science will continue to move on and self correct.

Religion has no such function without barbarity.

As for religion, it is up to religion to prove itself. Very little about religious spirituality is provable or testable! In my opinion Science has proven itself in a very logical and reliable way, where religion has not.

(8)

Morality

> *"I'm an Atheist, and that's it. I believe that there's nothing we can know except that we should be kind to each other and do what we can for each other."*—Katharine Hepburn (1909-2003) Actress, in Ladies Home Journal (October 1991)

Are you a moral person? I believe that I am a moral person. I care for my family, I volunteer and do work for various charities, I pay my taxes just like you, I tell my wife I love her at least three times a day, and I am honest in my dealings in the world of business. I stand up to be counted on issues like global warming, the rights of minorities and the rights of others around me.

I believe that I have the ability to act in a moral manner by walking away from one of the dearest relationships I have ever experienced because the people in that institution continue to cause abuse to others. Leaving the Anglican Church of Canada was one of the hardest things I have ever done, and yet I did it on the strength of moral principle.

Should I be moral because I want to please God? Should I be moral because I fear hell? No! There are better reasons for morality, like caring for others and looking out for my kin. If I were moral only because I fear the wrath of God, I would be a nasty person. What would this say about God if it were really true?

I used to think God was omnipotent (all powerful) and omniscient (all knowing). If this is the case, why hasn't God stepped in to prevent the damage we do to one another? I do not accept biblical versions of the answer to this question since they are full of looped logic and myths, if you want to prove this point to me you had better be prepared to present clear logic, not dogma.

If God, in all his majesty, was to step into our world and educate us we would have no problem listening. We would lay down all of our weapons and listen as it would be obvious that God was speaking. God would need only to stay with us for our continued understanding. Imagine! God living with us! As amazing as this seems, we would still have free will!

But God is not here (or perhaps he is not capable of being here). Meanwhile, those who are supposed to be the most enlightened, the ones closest to God, gloss over the heinous crimes against humanity perpetuated by their religions.

While those who believe in a God are able to act kindly to one another, very often they do not. In fact, our unwillingness to relinquish dogmatic beliefs is often at the root of our violence towards one another.

I act in a moral manner towards others because I care deeply about the world I live on. I care about the people on my world. I hope you will be moral towards me for the same reason.

(9)

End of A letter to My Curious Friends

> *"One of the proofs of the immortality of the soul is that myriads have believed in it. They have also believed the world was flat."*—Mark Twain (1835-1910), in Notebook

    The sun is about 26,000 light-years from the center of the Milky Way Galaxy, which is about 80,000 to 120,000 light-years across, and less than 7,000 light-years thick. We are located on one of its spiral arms, out towards the edge. It takes the sun, and our solar system, roughly 200-250 million years to orbit once around the Milky Way. In this orbit, we, and the rest of the Solar System, are traveling at a velocity of about 250 km/sec. That is about 900,000 km/h!

    We are traveling so fast right now that we cannot begin to comprehend it without mathematics. Even then it is somewhat outside of our ability to understand our speed in real terms.

    Our planet has existed for billions of years, in a galaxy that has billions of stars in it. The universe has billions of galaxies. We have had ample time to evolve to who we are and we have had ample time to meet our maker.

    Why isn't any of this in the Bible? Isn't it supposed to be the inspired word of our creator?

    After I watched the jet airliners crash into the world trade centre on Sept 11th 2001 I realized how "tribal" our species can be. Christians, while presently much more moderate, are no more innocent than Islam when it comes to the perpetuation of terror. Most of this is because the large majority of us are ideologically opposed to any compromise of our belief system. When are we going to give up believing in myths and start to deal with the reality of who we are as a species?

If humankind is going to progress we had better get our heads out of the sand, look up to the stars, and understand where we are. Once we have gained a real situational perspective we can begin to solve the problems associated with our existence. The first problem we have is that we do not seem able to cooperate. What is it that hinders our ability to cooperate? Dogmatism plays a large role. Democracy and good trade relations go far in solving these problems.

Twice now, I have been accused of being "arrogant" because I have left the Christian faith. One of the men who calls me arrogant is quite unwilling to learn, because he thinks he already has all of the answers he needs written in a book that was compiled 1680 years ago. I honestly believe he has it wrong. It's too bad he won't listen to the arguments presented by science and by reason. I have listened to both sides of the arguments. There is so much depth to the argument that science provides, how can we ignore it?

Here we are, lowly humans, only recently evolved from primates, wanting for certainty where there is none. Should we to accept a shortcut rather than the long road to a deeper understanding of ourselves? We could walk down the same road as those before us and never know the difference.

No.

Instead we need science to light our way. The hope that we derive from a deeper understanding of ourselves and our universe will shine like a beacon for generations to come.

Jeff Olsson

p.s. I hope that all of you will still consider me to be a friend, even though I hold beliefs contrary to your own.

(10)

Watching TV

"I'm a born again atheist."—Gore Vidal, Writer

I will never forget the day I became an atheist. It was an amazing experience.

It was a snowy day in early January of 2003 and I had just finished moving a pile of furniture around the living room of our new home. Tired, sweating and with an ice cold drink in hand I flipped on the television. The onscreen channel guide from our new digital cable box presented me with a number of TV evangelists to choose from. In Canada we have a lot of televangelists on TV.

A name that I recognized caught my eye and I stopped at "This Is Your Day", featuring Benny Hinn on Visions TV. Benny is the just the sort of preacher who claims that God can heal you through his ministry.

"Perfect!", I thought.

I had seen Benny before when he was on TV in a documentary by HBO. I suppose the documentary story was what drew me to find out what Benny had to say.

Thinking I was quite alone I blurted out, "I just don't believe this". From around the corner and down the hall my wife yelled "What? What don't you believe?"

"The size of this mans comb-over" I replied.

Within moments the whole family was standing in the living room gawking at the TV. The hair on Benny's head waved at us twice for each turn or nod of his head. Swish Swish ... I have since heard my family refer to that historic moment in time as "The comb over catastrophe of 2003."

It was the hairdo that killed my faith! Talk about a bad hair day.

There I sat, with an icy drink, and the cool concepts of disbelief and skepticism now firmly implanted into my psyche. At 39 years of age and for the first time in my life, I was ready to watch Christian television as it should be watched.

As the show progressed Benny sat with others in lavish chairs in a semi circle facing the camera, I couldn't believe the quantity of viewer letters piled up in front of Benny! Does he actually get that many letters? There were so many that they packed them into bails and shipped them on pallets.

He preyed over whole palette loads of letters all at once, asking for god's healing for all of those people. Next, he cherry picked a letter out of a pile and read it aloud. It was from a lady who was experiencing difficulty breathing. As he held his hand out towards the camera he said a prayer for the lady. He asked both the lady (and me) to pray along with him. "Hold your hands out!" I held my hand out and nodded my head in prayer. His hair continued to mesmerize me. Swish, was it actually waving at *me*? How could I know for sure?

He had commanded her lungs to loosen and explained that I could have a similar healing if I would just believe. Trying to imagine that lady, located somewhere in North America, perhaps sitting on her sofa in another city. I envisioned her finding relief as her lungs began to function properly. Wouldn't it be nice to actually believe that she really got better? I really wanted to believe but something 'swish' was nagging at me.

Benny tied up the prayer nicely by explaining that I should send a small amount of "seed money" to show my faithfulness. By sending in money I could experience the blessing of doing Gods works amongst his people.

I whispered, "I don't believe that either." It was then that I fully realized that my wife and children were still watching television with me.

For a moment I was paralyzed by the notion of disbelief... and then I began to think about what I had just said, and why I knew I must be right.

On that day I learned that Atheists are much more than just people who don't believe in a particular god, they are people first. We have more than one dimension. We care about people. We have families, friends, aspirations and things we just like to do for fun. Our political views vary greatly. And we are not afraid to think for ourselves. Generally we are well educated and we serve our communities in a whole variety of ways.

Ok, so atheists are people first, are we merely people who don't believe in a particular version of god?

(11)

Atheoi

"I have never seen what to me seemed like an atom of proof that there is a future life."—Mark Twain (1835-1910), from Albert Bigelow Paine's Mark Twain; A Biography

You may find it odd but the atheism that we know today is a relatively new phenomenon, even though disbelief has certainly been around for thousands of years.

The name atheist or atheoi was used to describe the godless in Saint Paul's letter to the Ephesians, Chapter 2:12. The most common translation of atheoi is "those who are without god." By this, Saint Paul refers specifically to those who are without the Christian God. Any non Christian was referred to in this manner! Sadly, the word is used in a negative context. Apparently we lack hope in this world without the Christian God in it. I guess they forgot to tell some of us that part.

Not only has the term atheoi been used in a negative sense, it has also been used in a pejorative sense. Anyone who failed to believe in the God of any Abrahamic religion seems to have been called "godless" even when they believed in their own particular god.

Muslims were godless to the Christians; Christians were godless to the Jews etc. The old version of the Good Friday rite in the Catholic prayer book referred to the "faithless Jews" in recognition of the fact that they do not believe in Christ.

This term was finally removed because it was construed to be pejorative and was changed to a less demeaning phrase by Pope John XXIII in 1960. Perhaps he was worried about the use of words that could so easily be misconstrued to be similar to what Hitler had said in some of his speeches. (The term 'perfidia iudaica' means faithless Jews, while the term 'perfidis iudaica' means "Jews betray" or "Jews are treacherous in character")

In the Anglican tradition the old prayer books stated:

> "MERCYFULL God, who hast made all men, and hatest nothyng that thou hast made, nor wouldest the deathe of a synner, but rather that he should be converted and live; have mercy upon all Jewes, Turkes, Infidels, and heretikes, and take from them all ignoraunce, hardnes of heart, and contempt of thy word: and so fetche them home, blessed Lorde, to thy flocke, that they maye bee saved among the remnant of the true Israelites, and be made one folde under one shepeherde, Jesus Christ our Lord; who lyveth and reigneth . . ."

I have tried many times to see how this verse could be read in way that is not derogatory. Each time I've tried I faced the gloomy assertion made in the statement "but rather that he should be converted and live". It literally means that God would rather save us than be forced into killing us for our non belief. It's tough to see how we deserve to die In the first place. Scripture says God is invisible (spirit), and yet that God is the one who expects us to 'believe or else', according to this passage. Am I really hard hearted? Am I wrong to try to make a better world for myself the best way I know how?

In the United Kingdom, under the blasphemy law it was illegal to deny the existence of God. Atheists, Unitarians and others had been jailed under this law from the 1600s until the mid 1920's. There were even some who spent their last days living in a UK prison because they had been bold enough to speak or write about their beliefs.

Protests and Public outrage occurred as the last person to be incarcerated for blasphemy was jailed in December of 1921. John William Gott, a trouser salesman, had three previous convictions for publishing pamphlets called Rib Ticklers. Oddly, the pamphlets were full of advertisements for men's trousers and cartoons that asked questions about God that were intended to challenge

Priests on various issues. They portrayed Jesus as a clown riding on the back of two donkeys, referring to the Biblical story (Matthew 21) of his reentry to Jerusalem. Gott had a known incurable illness when he was incarcerated. He died shortly after his sentence ended.

After Gott's sentencing there were numerous attempts to use the law but none succeeded. Either it was misapplied to Islam (it was written specifically for Christianity) or was used where other laws such as the theatres act already had jurisdiction. In one case following the reading of the poem *The Love that Dares to Speak its Name* by *James Kirkup* on the front steps of St. Martin's in the Fields, a trial would have meant that numerous people, including some MPs would have been called as witnesses or face prosecution had it been successful. In March 2008 the *Blasphemy Law* in the United Kingdom was finally abandoned by an act of parliament, with the full agreement of the Archbishop of Canterbury, who personally urged that it be repealed in a television interview.

Karen Armstrong, a former Catholic nun who wrote a number of books on comparative religion asserted, "During the sixteenth and seventeenth centuries, the word 'atheist' was still reserved exclusively for polemic . . . The term 'atheist' was an insult. Nobody would have dreamed of calling *himself* an atheist."

It seems there will always be people who do not believe in each others gods. Today the average atheist seems to take this idea a small step further by not believing in any of the numerous gods that have been enshrined throughout history. Essentially two main categories of atheism seem to have emerged; there are implicit atheists, and there are explicit atheists.

(12)

Atheism Is More Than a Word

"It was, of course, a lie what you read about my religious convictions, a lie which is being systematically repeated. I do not believe in a personal God and I have never denied this but have expressed it clearly. If something is in me which can be called religious then it is the unbounded admiration for the structure of the world so far as our science can reveal it."—Albert Einstein (1879-1955), in his biography Albert Einstein: The Human Side

In his book titled "The Case Against God", George Smith introduces the idea of **Implicit Atheism** which describes the beliefs of those who have spent little or no time thinking about the concept of God. Many implicit atheists will not claim to know much about God at all. They have no readily formed defense against religious assertions made to them except to go on as if they did not hear, as they do with most of the religious ideas that they may hear.

On the other hand, **Explicit Atheism** is where a person knows about, has examined and still rejects the concept of a god. Many modern atheists in this category reject the supernatural for scientific reasons. Rejection of the concept of god usually occurs along with the rejection of other mythical creatures like unicorns, fairies, goblins, demons, or ghosts. Explicit atheists usually have a number of logical arguments "armed and ready" to be used in defense of their own belief system.

Thomas Jefferson summed up this concept well in the following statement:

> *"I have recently been examining all of the known superstitions of the world, and do not find in our particular superstition (Christianity) one redeeming feature. They are all alike, founded upon fables and mythologies."*—**Thomas Jefferson** (1743-1826), in a letter to Dr. Woods

To be truthful, Jefferson rejected all religion, but still believed there was a god. Deists believe that there most likely is a God even though they withhold from attaching any attributes to it. Some deists pray, some do not. Jefferson could have been called an explicit Deist, (as opposed to an implicit Deist), for the same reasoning that applies to implicit and explicit atheism.

I am merely one of the many atheists who come from former (deeply) religious lives. When I was younger, I served as an Anglican priest for more than 10 years. I spent a good portion of my life studying scripture, learning and using the liturgies. I had practiced Christianity for over 30 years before I finally came to unbelief. I was a charismatic Christian and was baptized in the Holy Spirit, spoke in tongues, and I believed in God for miracles. Now, I clearly fit into the category of explicit Atheism. I know *why* I do not believe.

Some of my Christian friends are perplexed by the idea that I would or could walk away from my religious faith. I have learned a lot on my journey away from a life based only on belief. I gradually became so sure of myself that I felt I had to leave the ministry, and eventually Christianity.

(13)

How do I know?

"I don't know"—Homer Simpson

How do I know?

How does anyone know?

It's quite common for people to say that they are certain there is a god; while some say they are certain there isn't a god. How is it possible to "know" such a thing? I am always perplexed when strong opinions on any such matter are expressed. Why is it that two people looking at the same information can come to two totally different conclusions, where one believes a supernatural event has happened and one does not?

There are a number of ways in which we can gain knowledge; my experience has been that once we become aware of *how* we gain knowledge, we become better learners.

"Tenacious knowledge" or the "method of tenacity" refers to information that has been accepted as true because it has always been believed to be true or because superstition supports it. When I was young my mother would tell me never to swallow my chewing gum because it would stay in my stomach forever. Eventually, she said, my stomach would be full of gum and I would starve with no room for food. I thought it was better to be safe than sorry, (and that's how Pascal's bubble gum wager was born.) I always spit my gum out when done with it. Apparently my buddies' parents had told them this story too, and their parent had in turn heard it from their parents.

There are a number of pitfalls associated with knowing things by ***tenacity*** that include:

a) The transfer of information that is just not true.
b) Information that comes from a source that was initially reliable but has now disappeared, never to be verified.
c) Information for which the origin is based in superstition

Perhaps there really was a time when gum could get stuck in your stomach . . . But somehow I doubt it was ever true.

This does not mean that knowledge that is tenacious is necessarily incorrect, even if it is suspect. Habit plays a role in the way this type of information is transferred and acquired (gossip, superstition) and the way that it is used.

Advertisers take advantage of habit by repeating their claims again and again until enough people accept the claims as true. Habit and the way we think about the world plays a large role in what we come to believe about the world.

The method of knowing called ***intuition*** is also commonly used where knowledge is accepted as true because it "feels right".

There is a large risk of being wrong when using intuition, based on numerous cognitive behavioral, probability, belief, social and memory biases.

On its own intuition can serve us well, but we humans are prone to a selective memory bias in which we remember the hits and forget the misses. Therefore we tend to remember when intuition has worked well for us and forget when it has failed. The problem with this method of knowing is that there is no readily definable way to sort out true information from untrue information. Deciding what to make for lunch is a decision that often falls into the "feels right" category. Would it be wise to use this method to decide on where to invest in the stock market? I don't think so.

Through intuition humans have come to a number of crazy conclusions. Accusations of witchery during the middle ages were based on intuition and often involved a confused or gullible witness who would attest to the most outlandish version of events. A recent news story reported a sad example of what can happen when intuition coupled with ignorance run amok:

—From the May 21st, 2008 MSNBC story *"Kenya mob reportedly burns 11 'witches' Police say locals accused women and men of 'bewitching' their children."*

It is unlikely that we will never know if these actions were caused by tenacity or intuition alone or if there was an authority figure behind the mob urging them onward.

(14)

Authority

Jesus said to him, "I am the way, the truth, and the life. No one comes to the Father except through Me. "If you had known me, you would have known my father also; and from now on you know him and have seen him." Philip said to him, "Lord, show us the father, and it is sufficient for us."
—John 14:6-8

The method of knowing by **authority** relies on information or answers from an expert in a particular subject area. This method can be highly accurate in some cases, but leaves one open to manipulation and outright falsehood.

Face it, we normally rely on experts for a lot of the decisions we make in life.

But, do we ask the hard questions to determine how *they* know what they are talking about? If an investment adviser was to knock on your door tomorrow, would you ask to see her credentials? How would you know that the stocks or mutual funds she is brokering are actually earning interest as well as she says they are?

The use of authority as a means of information often works best where information is available from *other* authorities working in the same field as your authority. This way the public and can access an alternate source by which to verify information.

Recently a friend challenged me on my unbelief (I have no problem with that, that's what friends do) she said she trusts her pastor's beliefs because he has a PhD in theology and he has been in the clergy for 40 years.

I asked her if she knows what you learn when you study theology. She did not. I didn't have the heart to tell her that theology is not a study of 'whether or not' god exists. It is a study of the system of religion, what influenced it as it evolved and the nature of religious truths. (Why is a sacrament a sacrament? Why do Christians think Jesus is the son of god and not his cousin?). Authority is also the system of knowing that is used when the person in charge has power to exert beliefs onto a population.

(15)

Tenacity, Faith and Authority

"A belief is a lever that, once pulled, moves almost everything in a person's life"—Sam Harris in The End of Faith

The method of knowing called **faith** is a variant of the method of authority in which people have an unquestioning trust in the authority figure, text or idea and therefore accept the information without doubt or challenge.

In all three of the Abrahamic religions, adherents are encouraged to use faith as means by which they can know God, please God and obtain a guarantee of eternal life. Christian scriptures that make these points include Romans 4:9-17 "Abraham's faith was credited to him as righteousness." Hebrews 11:6 "without faith, it is impossible to please God" and John 3:16 "whoever believes in him shall not perish".

Faith creates a psychological circumstance where an idea, text or claim that cannot be verified can become "truth" to a large number of people. Faith becomes knowledge. The popular idea that faith is a virtue encourages people not to criticize. The methods of tenacity and authority also play a large role in creating this circumstance in human populations. Used together, the trinity of tenacity, authority and faith can become an unstoppable force for the creation and acceptance of irrational or erroneous, religious, even militaristic beliefs, especially when circumstances are correct.

If you struggle with what I am saying, that the church encouraged faith for this reason, read the words of our church father St, Augustine for yourself. In chapters 20 and 21 of the *online version* you can see how St. Augustine rationalizes this idea. The idea that "faith becomes knowledge" is exactly what St. Augustine is talking about in chapter 20. He also goes on to discourage inquisitiveness in chapter 21. When I read a different translation of this text for the first time many years ago I literally stopped in my tracks. I realized that the concept of religion as a method of controlling a population was not only plausible; it was an ancient technique that had been reproduced many times over the ages. My preaching changed dramatically as a result, it was one of my early steps toward a more liberal, peaceful and inclusive faith.

St. Augustine is well renowned for the creation of the theology of 'just war' and the concept of 'original sin'. It is important to note how powerful an influence these two concepts have had on Christianity. Would Jesus have lead troops to war? Many say he never would have. Did Jesus ever speak of original sin? (No!) Were you actually born into sin? None of these terms exist in any of the biblical scriptures! Imagine what Christianity would have been like, as it played out over the centuries, without the concept of original sin or just war. It would have been much tamer, kinder and inclusive. Sadly, a tame, kind and inclusive religion cannot be used to control a population.

More examples of tenacity, authority and faith used as methods of knowing "truth" can be found by studying the *Cargo Cults* formed after periods of exploration and contact with indigenous tribes and during the Second World War in Melanesia, Micronesia, New Guinea and other pacific countries. Primitive cultures living on islands were introduced to missionaries, modern explorers or military forces and assumed that they were spiritual or godlike beings because of the apparent 'super' powers that the newcomers possessed. In Journeys To The Past, David Attenborough, explains that the first time a cult of this type "sprang up" was in Fiji in 1885 and then again in 1932.

"With the increasing spread of western materialism through the pacific, the cults increased in number and frequency. Anthropologists have noticed two separate outbreaks in New Caledonia, four in the Solomons, four in Fiji, seven in the New Hebrides and over fifty in New Guinea, most of them being quite independent and unconnected with one another. The majority of these religions claim that one particular messiah will bring the cargo when the day of apocalypse arrives."

This mixture of Christianity, taught by missionaries, ancient beliefs and 'cargoism' were formed as islanders were unable to acquire the materials and equipment similar to that being delivered to their white visitors. Consequently the cult members incorporated symbols from the outside culture into their religious beliefs. The intent was to gain the powers of the outsiders by mimicking their behaviours, beliefs and equipment.

Villagers watched the white people who sat at desks, did no real work, listening to small boxes that emitted strange voices, and noticed that the cargo frequently came to these people. In some cases it came by ship and in others it was dropped from the sky. It also seemed clear to these people that the cargo was supernatural in origin. They had lived for centuries on an island on which there were no minerals other and rock, plant fiber and wood. How could any mere human possibly have made an enamel refrigerator, teacup, steel machete or kerosene lamp? They also noticed that the white visitors did not make this cargo themselves.

And so it was that they set out to mimic the behaviour of the visitors in order to get the Gods to bring cargo for them. They incorporated knowledge gained through flawed guesswork when watching the outsiders (intuition) and listening to their own leaders like Nambas, whom I will introduce later (an authority). And of course there was a core set of beliefs on which the cult members acted out in faith

Anthropologists tell stories about cults who have built mock airstrips complete with mock radar towers, bamboo aircraft and wooden radios with coconut headphones. They religiously watched their posts thinking that the imitation of the US military's behavior would attract the same cargo, dropped from the sky when the soldiers first arrived 50 years prior. Some of the cults that formed during the 1940's persist as adherents religiously wait for the return of the original soldiers, thought to be Gods, who first brought the cargo to their islands.

In Guns Germs and Steel, Jared Diamond tries to answer the questions of one New Guinean man named Yali, with whom he walked down a beach for an hour, one day in 1972. As they walked on the sand and chatted Yali asked "Why is it that you white people developed so much cargo and brought it to New Guinea, but we black people had little cargo of our own?" The thesis of Diamond's book is an attempt to answer that question. Diamond states: "History followed different courses for different peoples because of differences among people's environments, not because of biological differences among peoples themselves"

There is no reason to think that people who are members of a cargo island "culture" are stupid or unable to learn. In fact, IQ tests written by their children (now in modern schools) show them to have an IQ that may slightly exceed yours or mine. Instead, because of the environment in which they have grown up they lacked the framework by which to interpret an event such as white humans landing in large aircraft and dropping cargo. Today the main difference between mainstream culture and theirs is that we come from a society that has a rather complete knowledge of how aircraft work, how the military operates, both from school and from watching movies and television. It's not mysterious to us. Happenings that you and I would see as reasonable or rational, based on our culture, seemed quite mystical and magical to the New Guinean of 1932.

Once 'written' into their culture this mysticism has persisted and strings of erroneous belief continued as the religion quickly evolved. The *John Frum Cult* on an Island called Tanna has persisted and stabilized since the Second World War. Cult devotees await the return of an American serviceman whom they believe to be named John Frum. The followers believe that John Frum will one day return to the island and take his people away, ushering in a new age of prosperity and happiness. *(A Feb, 2006 story and photographs from Smithsonian Magazine are available at Smithsonian.com)*

In Journeys To The Past, Attenborough ties this all together nicely when he tells the story of a conversation between himself and a John Frum cult devotee named Sam. In this story Attenborough asks Sam why, after nineteen years he is still waiting for John Frum to come back. It seems that waiting nineteen years is an awfully long time to wait for someone.

Sam responded by turning the question around, and he did so in a way that defended his own religious beliefs quite brilliantly when he asked Attenborough why it was ok to wait for Jesus for two thousand years, when Jesus still does not return. It made waiting for John Frum seem like a cakewalk.

The explanation of how cargo cults formed shows how flawed intuition and a lack of certain specific knowledge can help a religious movement to start. Sam's statement shows us how faith keeps the religion going over the years.

However, authority also plays a role and Attenborough also tells an interesting story about Nambas, one of the cult's leaders.

Nambas was an innovator in this religion, not a follower. Nambas had a radio and would listen for messages from John Frum. These messages would in turn be passed along to followers who would take them to heart and partake in what they were told to do. When David Attenborough came to visit him Nambas claimed that he already knew Attenborough was coming because John Frum had warned him by radio. While the followers were impressed, Attenborough knew that they had sent word to Nambas when he first arrived, and that for two weeks his intention to visit was known. A Catholic missionary explained to Attenborough that the radio in fact was an old woman with piece of scrap electrical wire wrapped around her waist. She would fall into a trance behind a screen in Nambas hut and begin to talk gibberish. Nambas would interpret this to his followers.

As it turned out, Nambas was turning the gibberish it into whatever stories he liked, and claiming that it came from a God named John Frum. As the highest authority in his religion the followers listened carefully to what he said, and many were impressed by his abilities. It appears that **tenacity**, **faith** and **authority** have worked well in this case, almost as well as it has in Christianity.

(16)

Rationalism

Reason and free inquiry are the only effectual agents against error.
—*Thomas Jefferson, Notes on the State of Virginia, 1787*

But what about other ways of learning?

The *rational* method of knowing seeks answers by the use of logical reasoning. Reason is used as a tool to solve problems, find flaws in nonsense claims or to create a strategy by which to accomplish goals. The use of rational thought is far superior to the acceptance of dogma or non testable claims.

One of the pit falls of the rational method is that logic, on its own, when not based on verifiable truths, can fail when one of the assumptions made is either inaccurate or false. In addition to this problem, logical fallacies can create an error caused by faulty reasoning itself.

One of my favorite shows has always been Monty Python. I remember staying up late on Saturday evenings to watch it on CBC as a child. Later when my children were still young we would re-enact scenes in our own way and video tape the skits, replay them and watch mom laugh out loud. We performed our own versions of these skits in the basement on cold winter days.

"The Argument Clinic" was one such skit that inspired us. In one of my favorite versions a customer would go to the clinic, fail to pay and try to get an argument for free.

Dad: "Krista, you are not allowed to argue unless you've given me 5 dollars first."
Krista: "I just gave you 10 dollars"
Dad: "Bollox!"
Krista: "Mom, Dad said Bollox again, I don't want to argue about money I want a real argument" (points finger in Dad's face)
Dad: "But you didn't give me my money!"
Krista: "Gotcha! If I didn't give you money, why are you arguing?"
Dad: "I'm not arguing."
Krista: "Yes you are, and if you're arguing I must have given you the money!"
Dad: "I could be arguing for fun, like I do with your mother!"
Krista: "Bollox!"
Dad: "Mom, Krista said Bollox again! . . . Now give me the money."

As you can see one of the characters in this play is lying about having paid and is employing a logical fallacy to get a free argument. This skit uses an inference rule that states that if A is true, and A implies B, then B is also true. "If you're arguing I must have given you the money!"

Again, rationalism works well when the assumptions at the root of the reasoning are factual. This is one of the reasons why the scientific process is powered by the use of rational thought and relies on a mixture of rational thinking and empiricism.

(17)

Empiricism

"Why continue? Because we must. Because we have the call. Because it is nobler to fight for rationality without winning than to give up in the face of continued defeats. Because whatever true progress humanity makes is through the rationality of the occasional individual and because any one individual we may win for the cause may do more for humanity than a hundred thousand who hug their superstitions to their breast."
—Isaac Asimov

Empiricism uses observation or direct sensory experience to obtain knowledge; it occaisionally contradicts the other forms of "knowing", and is criticized because it most often relies only on our five direct senses to obtain knowledge.

When combined, rationalism and empiricism, known as *the scientific method* form the most accurate method of gaining knowledge that mankind has ever developed. The greatest discoveries ever found have come to humans through this method. For example, prior to the use of the scientific method of knowing it was common for large percentages of all populations (mostly young children) to die from waterborne diseases before the introduction of potable water systems. There is no question, even when you factor in all of the modern wars; fewer people have died as a result of recent scientific discoveries. Science saves lives.

The Science Channel currently has a *Big 100* list of the greatest scientific discoveries of all time. In this collection of stories you will find these many examples of how important science has been to us as a race. Here are my favorite examples of empiricism:

- Bacteria were discovered by a Dutch lens grinder Anton Van Leeuwenhoek, in 1683, after scraping a white paste off the teeth of a man who had never once cleaned his teeth. He discovered these "animacules" when he saw them for the first time using a microscope he built a number of years earlier.
- An early understanding of Photosynthesis in plants was discovered when Jan Ingenhousz, (1770) noticed that green plant parts gave off bubbles in sunlight but not in the shade, where other plant parts do not give off bubbles at all.
- Earths inner core was discovered after an earthquake in New Zealand when a Danish seismologist noticed that her stations showed that seismic waves would reflect back at a frequency that did not fit the mathematical model of a solid earth (1936). Inge Lehman was a pioneer among women and scientists.
- Plate tectonics, where the earth's surface is broken into several large plates of rock that shift over time (a few inches per year). These plates crash into one another, shift about and slide to cause earthquakes volcanoes and mountains. Plate tectonics was discovered by many scientists working together since the 1960's.
- Potential for life in earth's early atmosphere was shown when elements in a container were exposed to electric discharge, creating organic compounds by Stanley Miller, 1953.
- The classification of all species was developed by Carl Linnaeus and is still in use today, quite an accomplishment considering it started in 1735.
- A "mother lode" of Cambrian fossils was unearthed in the Canadian Rockies and provides a glimpse of what life was like on earth 500 Million years ago.
- "On the Origin of Species by Means of Natural Selection" published by Charles Darwin, in 1858 has become the underpinning theory behind

many fields of science, not the least of which are, biology, microbiology, zoology, medicine and others.

Empiricism works, and because people can reproduce experiments they do not need faith to believe something works. Empiricism allows you to "test and see for yourself" rather than accept information based on faith.

(18)

Flashes of Light—finding our inner bias

> *"I would love to believe that when I die I will live again, that some thinking, feeling, remembering part of me will continue. But as much as I want to believe that, and despite the ancient and worldwide cultural traditions that assert an afterlife, I know of nothing to suggest that it is more than wishful thinking."*—Carl Sagan (1934-1996), in The Demon Haunted World

Why it is that two people looking at the same information can come to two different conclusions, where one believes a supernatural event has happened and one does not?

The answer to that question lies in where and how each individual decides *when* to use the various methods of knowing. Most often this is done out of habit. Those habits are likely reinforced by the culture you choose to live in. Any person who relies heavily on tenacity, authority or faith as reliable methods of gaining knowledge is bound to get different answers than a person who gives more weight to rationalism and empiricism.

What is your predisposition?

I love visiting the restaurants at the Forks Market in downtown Winnipeg. Last May while we were having a treat, an old friend spotted me sitting in the restaurant. She hadn't seen me in at least five years and thought it would be nice to pop over and say hello. During the course of the conversation she told me (and my friends) that while visiting a synagogue she had seen a marvelous flash of light cross the room and come towards her. She said she "felt" the light penetrate her "very being."

To her the flash of light event has justified a deeply held religious belief that God is real and active in the physical world. I thanked her for telling me the story, and remarked that the experience "must have been quite special." We had many kind words and I encouraged her in her pursuit of a ministry as a priest. "Make sure you know what you intend to do as a minister" I told her. "Have a clear picture of how you intend to serve the people you love, go in with a plan." I do feel that she will do well; she is quite caring and able to show great empathy.

Clearly, her intention in telling me this story was to make me stop and think about the possibility that God is active in this world, *and that is just fine by me*. I think I owe it to her to take the time to stop and think about his story.

How should I begin my analysis of this situation?

Should I:

1. Accept the story as true and believe that she has just had a revelation from God (Tenacity, Faith)
2. Ask the Rabbi of the synagogue or a Priest how to interpret this event and trust their decision (Authority, Faith)
3. Seek an answer in scripture (Tenacity, Authority, Faith)
4. Seek out scientific studies where physics and cognitive psychology have been considered, think it through and determine if I can find a rational explanation? (Authority, Rational, Scientific)
5. Become a scientist myself and set up an experiment to reproduce this event and test it? (Rational, Empirical, Scientific)

Which would you choose if you were me? Which feels right? Does it scare you a little to think that science may be able to fully explain what happened to her?

Does a solid empirical explanation automatically rule out the possibility that God was involved with this event? No, it just makes it much less likely.

If you give some thought to how you answered these questions you can probably comfortably identify your own predisposition. You may be predisposed to believe that this event was supernatural and accept answers 1 or 2 (or both).

You may be predisposed not to believe in the supernatural and accept answers 3, 4 or 5.

No doubt there are a number of you who would make use of the scientific method but still believe that there may be a God even if you don't agree that God was actually involved in this event.

Let's now suppose that after many hours of experimentation we fail to come to a reliable scientific conclusion. Would you push aside your predispositions and admit that you still *do not know* what actually happened when your friend saw the flash of light?

If we suppose, for whatever reason that God is involved, we then need to show God's actions explicitly. In other words we need to show clearly, in a testable way, in a repeatable way, that God's hand guided the light to your friend's eye. Why? Because she is asking me to make a *very* important life decision based on her assertion. She wants me to give up my current understanding of the world, and follow.

Even if we could show that a God was involved in this event, we would have to ask which god it was. We cannot simply assume that because the light shone through the window of a temple that it was the Abrahamic God.

Was it the invisible God written about in the Christian scriptures? Was it the one of the Gods of the Hindu's? Perhaps it was Thor and the glimmer of light was a reflection off of *Mjolnir* his beautiful golden hammer?

Finally, what was God trying to say to him? How do we know my friend interpreted the answer correctly?

Since I am not willing to trouble the Rabbi with a full scale scientific investigation in the synagogue I am left to seek out scientific studies where the physics of human vision and cognitive psychology have been considered, think it through and determine if I can find a rational explanation.

The explanation written by Doctor Jackson, an Ophthalmologist can be found in the PubMed online database. Read at least to page 50 where the author discusses radiations emanating from bright lights caused by the moist edges of eyelids.

Based on Dr Jackson's analysis of many similar events my personal speculation of what happened during this Flash of Light event is that it was completely natural in its origin.

My friend is a wonderful, sensitive and caring person who was moved by the beauty of the synagogue and the ancient service in which she participated.

Take a heightened emotional state, add a tear to the eye, and the light shining through the beautiful stained glass window would do all the work of a miracle when it was reflected off of her eyelid. There is no need to speculate any cognitive defect in a case like this.

There is no doubt in my mind that this event was beautiful and deeply moving to her and it confirmed for her that she should help others in this world. While I do not believe it was supernatural I am sure that this event was not a bad thing. I am glad that she is not prone to bigotry against other beliefs, races or creeds.

The vision of a cross in the sky, reportedly seen by Emperor Constantine could easily have been caused by a similar optical effect. I have often wondered if Christianity would even exist today were it not for such an illusion.

Every week in Christian churches all over the world, glossalalia (speaking in tongues) and its interpretation is seen as confirmation that the Holy Spirit is working through the individual. It shows that they are indeed "born again", touched by God and blessed with belief in the one true religion. Of course not all churches act this way, only about 10 million Americans belong to churches that specifically claim that speaking in tongues is necessary to call yourself "born again", while two hundred and four million people in the United States claim to be Christian, according to the government census taken in 2001.

For decades, Hindu believers have attested that the Lord Ganesha consumed the milk that they offered to him on a spoon in the temple in New Delhi. Now they have found that all of the Gods of the Hindu Pantheon seem to consume the milk when it is offered up on a spoon. (Apparently this happens as a result of capillary action, a natural process which causes movement of liquids when in contact with two adjacent surfaces)

Millions of Hare Krishna adherents believe that when they chant they tap into the spiritual energy of Rama (A god who is also called Krishna), and that they are experiencing a higher state of consciousness when they practice the repetition of the mantra. They 'feel' their connection with Rama.

Sikh's believe that the Guru Nanak, following divine guidance, used his hand to stop a stone that was sent rolling down a hill to kill him. His hand left a deep imprint on the stone. Now water flows out from behind it. This pool provided ample water for the villagers. A temple has been constructed at this site where worshippers give thanks for this miracle from God.

A good friend of mine asserts that the healthy lifestyle of the people involved in the Jehovah Witness religion is superior to that of other religions. He cites this as fact and as proof of the truthfulness of his religious beliefs. Now, even the natural is being claimed as proof of the supernatural.

In every case, adherents of a religion find ample evidence to sincerely believe that their religion is the true religion; no religion seems to have a monopoly on such supernatural claims.

Why then is it that many critics of science state that atheists are 'biased' when we assert that we can not really know the truth about god until the evidence is produced? To me one of the greatest aspects of scientific enquiry is that we are committed to withhold an opinion until we actually know a "truth" in a testable and reliable way.

Listen carefully to any scientist who is worth his salt and he will not claim a fact where there isn't one. He understands how chance can produce results and that chance needs to be accounted for before any serious assertions can be made. When the scientist starts to talk about theories and laws you will know the experiment is over and that they have empirical evidence.

In The Demon Haunted World, Science as a Candle in the Dark, Carl Sagan creates somewhat of a parable when he plays the role of a man who claims to have a dragon living in his garage. You become excited by the prospect of studying a real dragon since there have been so many tales of dragons but no dragon remains have ever been found.

You ask to see the dragon, and after some vague hand waving showing you where it is standing you are told "I neglected to mention she's an invisible dragon".

Still eager and full of anticipation you offer up other tests to capture physical evidence of the dragon and at every turn you are discouraged. When you attempt thermal imaging you are told, "it is heatless". When you try to spread flour on the floor you are told it leaves no footprints because "it floats in air", has no body (it's "incorporeal") and so on and so on.

Sagan's point quickly becomes clear, it is impossible to prove or disprove an invisible, heatless, floating, incorporeal *anything*!

Now let's talk about bias again. Should you remain agnostic about the existence of this dragon? At what point do you say I just don't believe it? When does it become plain silly? What kind of a claim can be made about anything where no physical tests are allowed?

To say that science is biased because it cannot accept that there is a dragon in your garage is to ignore that the claim of an invisible dragon was worthless to begin with. The same standard should be applied to any claim about an invisible God. We should ignore it until someone is willing to provide evidence.

(19)

Bumps in the night—Animism

"Mister Ed: What do you say we go out riding and pick up a couple of fillies?
Wilbur Post: I'm not a horse, remember?
Mister Ed: Too bad, we could have a ball double dating."
—Mister Ed, a show about a talking horse
that was popular in the 1960's

One of the computer technology guys that used to provide support to my work team would swear at my computer whenever it acted up. On occasion he would hit it and say that it was going to "computer hell" if it would not smarten up. He kept us all laughing when the situation could have been tense. Apparently computer hell was a room down the hall that was just hot enough to fry the chips on a mother board, but cool enough to leave the case intact so new parts can be installed and it can be upgraded.

The technique of swearing and whacking the side of the computer never really worked and the machine would end up in the shop time and again. I suspected that he was actually the one in computer hell, and that my computer was his tormentor. (It had a Heccubus III processor!) I cannot imagine what computer hell would feel like to a computer, but I am sure there is an error message that describes it quite well.

In 2004, Justin Barret further developed a theory about how humans find "agency" in both living and non animate objects, sounds and images. He makes the assertion that part of the reason people believe in gods, or demons, comes from the manner in which our minds, particularly our agency detection device functions. He also asserts that human agency detection devices tend to suffer from hyperactivity, making them prone to find agents around us, including supernatural ones, given fairly modest evidence of their presence. This tendency encourages the generation and spread of god concepts. Barret is a Christian who believes that a mind prone to finding God, being natural, must have been designed by God.

In a New York Times article entitled "Darwin's God", Barret defends his theism as he says, "Suppose science produces a convincing account for why I think my wife loves me—should I then stop believing that she does?"

To me the answer is simple; Leslie, my wife is standing right next to me. If I call her name she answers "Yes dear". But no amount of shouting summons God. Just because my agency detection says there must be a supernatural agent nearby it does not mean it is so.

In 1998 Douglas Adams, speaking at the Digital Biota conference at Cambridge University, gave a wonderful and unscripted speech about the concept "Is There an Artificial God". He tackled the idea of fortuitious human circumstance and belief in a world created just for us by comparing us to rain puddles.

In a short story about a 'thinking' rain puddle Adams notices how well the indentation in the ground fits him (the puddle). It fits him so well that he begins to think that the world was made just for him. Even as the puddle shrinks from the heat of the sun it always fits the hole in just the right way. The puddle "frantically" hangs on to the notion that the world was created especially for it, right up until it evaporates completely in the sun.

Adams description of a faith built on the appearance of lucky circumstance "the world fits me rather neatly" is an almost perfect analogy to my own faith experience early on in my life. I really thought that life was created just for me. I did this because I did not understand that we have evolved in this environment. Only the ancestors of ours whose bodies had adapted to this world survived. In reality I am a product of those who survived, all of the others died. Their puddles dried up.

As a child I remember waking up at night when bumps and creaks startled me. Once aroused I could not get past the idea that there was something (or someone) moving around in the house. My imagination did not have far to go in order to generate all kinds of terrifying ideas about what could be out there. When I called out for my mother and father one of them would come to my room and listen with me. I still remember my mom saying, "Hear that! That's just the wind", or "Hear that, that's your father snoring again!", as she patted my head and urged me to go to back sleep.

Her coaching is a good example of how authority can play a role in developing the knowledge that a child has about the world and how it operates. She taught my mind not to listen to the 'feeling' but instead to listen to the rational explanation. Frankly it worked quite well and with a little encouragement I eventually became a little expert who could name any sound I heard at night. Once named, the sounds were without the power to harm me. I felt had control and as a result I became a child who slept with the lights turned off.

But what about the kids who grew up during the ages before the enlightenment, whose mothers and fathers really did believe that spirits or gods lurked in darkened corners? They thought that demons had the power to actually move the things that went bump in the night. How did they get past the fear?

Attachment theory is a psychological and evolutionary theory that provides a framework for how humans interact. In children, attachment is expressed as children seek to stay near their parents. Securely attached children use their parents as a sort of home base from which they discover the world around them. Alan Stroufe and colleagues (1983) from the University of Minnesota noted that securely attached 12-18 month old infants functioned with more confidence than non-securely attached infants 2-3 years later.

Developmental theorists Erik (1902-1994) and Joan Erikson established that once securely attached, young children approach life with a basic trust, a sense that the world is predictable and reliable. Erikson also noticed that some adolescents forge an identity early on by transferring their parent's values and expectations to themselves.

It follows that securely attached children, taking on their parent's identity later in their development would accept information given to them as true when their parents tell it to them. They would accept that they were created by a certain god or that god works in the realm of the supernatural. Children are pre-programmed in a manner, with a bias for parental input. This has obvious benefits, but at least one pitfall.

While believing what our parents say is not necessarily a bad thing, it does illustrate *how* we can accept information that is without any basis in fact and think it to be completely reliable and true later in life, especially if that knowledge was comforting in the face of 'demons' that lurk under our beds.

The information gained from the trinity of faith, tenacity, and authority can easily be combined with information gained from our own errant agency detection and greatly influence us during their earliest stages of learning.

When children's minds are at their most vulnerable some of them are bombarded with complete nonsense by their parents and it seems to stick with them for the rest of their lives.

Thankfully, most parents see God as a loving and kind God and express this view to their children.

I remember one mother who taught in our Anglican parish Sunday school. She took it upon herself to go well beyond the curriculum and give graphic descriptions and warnings about demons and hell to the children. She would twist her face and lower the tone of her voice as she told the children stories of demons fighting for their souls. She would urge the children to pray for angels to come and save them from the demons.

A number of the other mothers complained bitterly about this woman, she became offended and took a leave of absence. She was sincere in her belief, not to be swayed. When I was finally in a position to act I thanked her for leaving and for deciding not to return. She took my cue and stormed out.

At the time, I wondered about the ethics of a person that would scare the wits out of a child, especially when a generous description of a loving and gentle God would be enough. Now I wonder if she was simply full of the nonsense that she had come to know through faith, tenacity, authority, her parents, and her own hyperactive agency detection. I suppose I'll never know.

When a child asks "where did I come from?" we should stick to what we know through science, explain what sex is, eggs, sperm. Tell them how molecules called DNA can copy, and how beings like us have evolved over the millennia.

We should teach our children the best methods of learning that we know of, and coach them on how to use those methods. I also think it is prudent for every young child to understand that *we do not know* if there is a God even though many people may claim to know. Children need to know that there is no empirical evidence what-so-ever that *any* God has played a role in the formation of the world.

To be an atheist or an agnostic is to be one of the few who say "We don't know yet", in the face of mobs of people who claim to have the answer.

> "Two roads diverged in a wood, and I—
> I took the one less traveled by,
> And that has made all the difference."
> —Robert Frost (1874-1963) American poet, who received four Pulitzer Prizes Source: The Road Not Taken

(20)

Morality Evolved

"It seems to me that the idea of a personal God is an anthropological concept which I cannot take seriously. I also cannot imagine some will or goal outside the human sphere ... Science has been charged with undermining morality, but the charge is unjust. A man's ethical behaviour should be based effectually on sympathy, education, and social ties and needs; no religious basis is necessary. Man would indeed be in a poor way if he had to be restrained by fear of punishment and hope of reward after death."
—Albert Einstein (1879-1955), in Religion and Science,"
New York Times Magazine (November 9, 1930)

I could see him sitting on top of Gary as I peered through the slats. The space under the stairs to my grade three homeroom was safe because *he* couldn't fit through the gap between the steps and the wall. The brute looked right at me as he punched Gary in the back of his little head. Thump, thump, Gary's brow ground into the crushed rock that covered our school yard. Speckles of blood formed on his face as the sharp edges of the rocks cut into his skin. I knew that if I did come out from under the stairs that "big kid" from Grade 6 was going to catch me and beat me too.

Only a minute or so before he attacked us we were peacefully walking home, laughing as we crossed the field we had played soccer earlier in the day. In the distance we heard our names called out as the big brute ran towards us. "Come 'ere you little fuckers". Just like a play out of a rugby game he lunged forward and caught Gary Winston by the leg. Books flew open and papers took flight. Gary hit the ground so hard that I thought he was going to break his face.

That bastard had the power to do whatever he wanted to us and he made sure we knew it. Tears came to my eyes as I heard Gary wincing in pain.

"Why can't he be like us?" I wondered, "Why does that big dummy feel like he has to hurt everyone, all the time?" I was scared and angry and wished I was bigger so I could go out there and save Gary. Part of me wanted to reason with him, part of me wanted to kill him, but I knew neither was actually an option. All I could do was to hide, watch and hope that he would tire of the situation.

As I look back at this event I realize that the feelings I felt were primal, rational and moral, they seemed to come from within my gut and from my head. I wanted to stop what that kid was doing and protect my friend. I knew what was right, but was powerless to do anything.

Does our morality come about as a function of the way our brains work, as preliminary scientific investigations seem to indicate, or does it come from an external source, a transcendent source higher than humans? Do I follow a moral code or do I simply use the wiring that has evolved in my brain to figure out answers to moral questions as I live out each day?

Perhaps my morality is based on my cultural background, where I observe societal norms and base my decisions on what others may think or feel about my behaviour. Perhaps my morality is learned from my parents and those around me.

This is complicated business.

Funk and Wagnalls Standard College Dictionary defines 'moral' as 'related to conduct or character from the point of view of right and wrong; concerned with the goodness or the badness of an action, character, disposition, etc.

To the Christian, Jew or Muslim, the definition of morality usually sounds something like this: 'to do good deeds out of a love for God, according to the principles and rules handed to us by God'.

In my former life as a Christian, morality was clearly linked up with the Ten Commandments, which I believed were handed down to Moses by God himself. I also followed scripture and used it (in part) as a moral compass to help make important decisions. My morality was directly linked to a want for salvation and eternal life in heaven and to avoid the penalty of eternal damnation. While

God's grace and forgiveness (for me) played a huge role in my reckoning, being a moral person was the least that I could do to ensure my success.

There can be no question about it, fear of eternal damnation and the guilty feeling that I experienced when I thought I had done wrong played a large role in many of the decisions I made in life. Leslie, my wife reminded me (yesterday) about the explanation I had used to convince her why we needed to get married 25 years ago. I had told her that I loved her and that I wanted to spend the rest of my life with her, but I also said that as common law partners, we were "living in sin" and that we needed to make things "right with God". As I look back at that explanation I realize that I needed to "feel" good about our relationship from more than a humanistic perspective. I needed to know that my relationship with her would not compromise my promise of eternal life. Fear was a factor in everything I did.

Today, I am an agnostic who leans towards atheism and prone to disbelief when it comes to the supernatural. I am faced with the question, "how is it possible to be moral or good?" I need to become aware of how I make decisions, to understand my own psychology, culture, and physiology in order to come to conclusions about the possibility that I can be a good person without religious thought. The 'feeling' of guiltiness for having done wrong has not changed for me, and I sense that it is much more than a simplistic religious interpretation of circumstance or the result of a supernatural communication between the holy spirit, soul and mind. Instead, it appears to me that guilt is a completely human, (perhaps mammalian), response to the cognitive dissonance caused by doing what we know we should not have done to someone else with whom we empathize. Evidence of this viewpoint has been found when observing communities of animals, where behaviour patterns similar to humans that exemplify guilt, altruism, and empathy have been pinpointed.

For a brief explanation of what has been found look here: *http://news.bbc.co.uk/2/hi/science/nature/3014747.stm*

To many of my religious friends I seem to have abandoned my connection to the one who makes it possible to be moral in the first place. Recently, one Catholic friend wrote to me and said, "Atheism cannot, of itself, support the notion of morals and so to be "moral" in the strict sense means to compromise one's atheism." He makes no bones about it; he thinks morality and atheism are incompatible. He honestly feels that the definition of morality is the property of Catholic faith to the exclusion of all other religions or beliefs. He believes it, but should I? Can I define morality for myself?

One of my favorite books on this matter, written by Michael Shermer, is called "The Science of Good and Evil", in which Shermer states, "To be a fully functioning moral agent, one cannot passively accept moral principles handed down by fiat. Moral principles require moral reasoning". It is because of my history with the Anglican Church, and my deep dissatisfaction with the conservative bishops, clergy and laity that I feel it necessary to agree with Shermer.

I need to become a fully functioning moral agent, capable of thinking for myself rather than to accept the status quo, especially when the status quo advocates bigotry in a variety of forms.

(21)

Moral Equipment

"As a Historian, I confess to a certain amusement when I hear the Judeo Christian tradition praised as the source of our present day concern for human rights . . . In fact, the great religious ages were notable for their indifference to human rights."
—Arthur Schlesinger, Jr., historian, in a speech at brown university (1989)

My intent in writing this chapter is not to create an encyclopedic manual on morality, (or immorality) but to address what *I* see as the large issues. Issues that need to see the light of day.

There are numerous studies that look at human behaviour and examine our ability to be empathetic, kind, altruistic (moral), and even more. One recent study by Dr. Decety and others from the University of Chicago shows rather conclusively that children between the ages of 7 and 12 are "hardwired" to feel empathy *and* to act morally. This means that these kids have the neurological equipment necessary to be moral just like you or I. While using an fMRI machine to scan the brains of children researchers found that the moral reasoning centers of the children's brains lit up when faced with a situation where moral reasoning was required. Children brains also lit up in areas where an empathetic response was appropriate while watching images of others experiencing something painful. "The programming for empathy is something that is "hard-wired" into the brains of normal children, and not entirely the product of parental guidance or other nurturing." said Decety.

There are also a few interesting psychological games that have recently been used in similar fMRI studies on adults, in which participants are encouraged to make a moral, ethical choice about how to act in an emergency while being scanned. I encourage you to try these scenarios out to see what you come up with before you read on.

The Rail Switch Scenario: Imagine that there is a trolley rolling down a set of tracks and a madman has tied six people to the track, five people are tied up down one leg of the track and one person is tied on the other side of a rail switch. You are standing by the switch and must choose whether you let the five die or switch the tracks and let the one die. What do you do?

1. Do nothing (Five people die)

or

2. Switch the switch (one dies but five live)

Think carefully about your answer, and jot it down before you read on. Don't try to rationalize it, just know that your answer is *your* answer.

The Bridge Scenario: Now imagine that there is a trolley rolling down a set of tracks and a madman has tied five people to the track. You are standing on a footbridge that crosses over the rails and know that a heavy weight can stop the train. There is a heavy man standing next to you on the bridge, if you throw the heavy man onto the tracks the train will certainly stop in time to save the five. What would you do?

1. Do nothing (Five people die)

or

2. Throw the heavy man off the bridge to stop the train (one dies but three live)

Joshua Greene, a neuroscientist and philosopher from MIT has taken these questions very seriously. Seriously enough to conduct fMRI studies of participants brains as they answer them. In all cases the scans show that there is a conflict between the emotional center of the brain and the cognitive centre of the brain while answering these questions.

In response to the switch scenario, most respondents say they **would** throw the switch and save five people.

In response to the bridge scenario most respondents say they **would not** throw the man off the bridge.

Greene posits that people give an opposite answer to the Switch and Bridge scenarios because, as the scans show, the thought of throwing someone off of a bridge is "emotionally salient" and that strong emotion plays a role in making moral judgments.

Now try this additional question: You are a mother with your child during the Second World War. You are hiding in your basement along with a number of other people. There are soldiers searching around outside your house. Your baby begins to cry and you know you will be found out and all of your group will be killed. The only thing you can do is to cover your baby's mouth, which will smother the child and it will die. Is it morally permissible to do this?

According to Greene, people that choose "Yes it's ok to smother the baby" exhibit a sharp increase in activity in portions of the brain associated with high-level functioning. All participants experience a conflict between a strong emotional response and a strong cognitive response that points in the opposite direction. Personally, I cannot imagine what it would be like to live through such an event, war is horrific.

On his *webpage* Greene explains that moral thinking is a mixture of emotional responses and rational reconstructions and that each of us have been shaped by our culture and our own biology. He says that by doing these studies he is attempting to understand how humans think, and to learn how we can think better.

There are leagues of scientists that come from the same school of thought, where they view morals and decision making as a neurological process that comes completely from the natural processes found within the brain. Greene and others show us that virtually everyone has the physical equipment necessary to make moral decisions and that it is a completely natural process.

One of the underlying assumptions made in this assertion is the idea that we evolved from a lower species of primate and that our human morality, altruism and ethics, comes as the result of changes that occurred in our brains as we became more advanced. The manner in which portions of each of our brains interact can create some eerily uniform decisions across a population living within a relatively uniform culture.

To me it is no surprise that humans make similar decisions in each of the trolley car scenarios even though we may not know exactly why we do, yet. The deeper questions are: How do we make such uniform decisions? What is it within each of us that enables such uniformity? I assert that these answers can be found by developing a deeper understanding of neuropsychological processes.

One day a friend of mind threw the keys to his new car over to me and insisted that I take it out for a spin. As I pulled away from the curb I was impressed by how much it handled just like my own car. The way it cornered, the minor lag after you press on the gas pedal followed by a burst of forward motion, was the same. His car was slightly larger and quieter, it even had different options than mine but it turned out that the drive train, engine and front suspension were exactly the same. They were made by the same manufacturer but were branded differently to increase sales. There is no wonder that it handled just like my car.

Why would the moral behaviour produced by your brain be that much different than mine, especially when you consider that your neurological equipment is almost identical to mine? Why should anyone expect my capacity to be moral would magically disappear when I stop believing in a god?

One of my Catholic friends asserted that I have benefited from thousands of years of Christian culture that have influenced my understanding of morality. At first blush this reasoning seemed to work for me, until I realized that he had forgotten about the humans who lived for hundreds of thousands of years before Christianity.

Did our ancestors act like immoral animals before the advent of Christianity? Were we reformed immediately after Christ's tomb was found empty? The obvious answer is that humans have been quite altruistic and moral for a long time, especially when we were living in small groups, where the wellbeing and survival of the group literally depended on the participation of every individual. Morality and survival are linked.

There is plenty of evidence that morality, ethics and general good behaviour has been defined hundreds (thousands?) of times in the cultures that formed outside of Christianity. Chinese texts in the Dàwènk u culture sites are over 4500-5000 years old and the morality of Chinese peoples is expressed as a part of the fabric of their culture. Stories, myths and legends abound worldwide and anyone who does a diligent study of history must come to the conclusion that morality and moral concepts exist outside of Christianity and they thrive.

When we sharpen our pencils and compare one group of humans to another we find small differences in *what* behaviours are considered to be moral. For example, the bulk of the 'moral' behaviours exhibited by Chinese people are quite similar to the behaviours exhibited by Americans or Europeans. We all care for our children, we fight for the rights of those whom we love, and we form political systems because we value a 'fair' society, we punish those who steal, and we admonish those who dishonor our elders. We codify what we consider to be important into laws. These laws are based on ancient ideas and assumptions about what is just and right and are sustained culturally by our elders and our religious leaders and are enforced by police or armies. We each have our own music, literature, lifestyle, painting and sculpture, theater and film in which we express these values in a manner that is meaningful to us. The difference is in *how* we do the things we do, not whether we do them. It is only when we look at the details that we see that the moral decisions made by various cultures are different.

Scientists who study and develop evolutionary psychology assert that all human cultures and behaviors are sculpted by the way the human brain processes information. Virtually every human brain, barring damage or birth defect, has a language acquisition module that will learn and interpret whatever language is being spoken to it. Accordingly, human cultures each have their own celebrated stories, rhymes, and songs, which are expressed with the primary intent of educating their young about that language. Each brain has the ability for intelligence and learning according to the limitations of its long term and short term memory and its ability to calculate in a variety of ways. Long before science was invented humans understood the necessity to repeat information until it 'stuck' in the brain of the child and to use repetitive rhymes to teach children.

Each brain has a sex-specific mating preference by which procreation or sex for pleasure can occur. A foraging mechanism enabling the search for sustenance, an alliance-tracking mechanism by which we determine who is on our side in a conflict, a cheater detection mechanism, a fear and protection mechanism and an incest avoidance mechanism.

We also have an agency detection mechanism that helps us to form a 'theory of mind' for people and animals. We often mistake agency in objects, shadows, noises or God concepts. The result of which has been the almost universal creation of supernatural belief in every culture. It stands to reason that every culture that exists today has similar features because the humans in each geographical area share similar features in the structure of their brains (and bodies). Human culture forms in and around us and is as much as expression of uniqueness as it is an expression of uniformity.

Humans are moral because they have the mental equipment to be moral. Those who were able to moral, prospered in small tribes and we are their descendants.

(22)

St. Augustine's Morality

"Say what you like about the Ten Commandments, you must always come back to the pleasant fact that there are only ten of them."
—H.L. Mencken, (1880-1956), editor and critic

Let's rewind a bit and look at St. Augustine's perspective on morality.

St. Augustine (354-430 CE) is considered a saint, pre-eminent doctor of the Catholic Church and patron of the Augustinian order. Whether you are Anglican or Catholic this mans writings play a large role in the formation of your theology and is expressed in your churches rites and creeds.

In *Of the Morals of the Church*, St. Augustine of Hippo, (388 CE) attempted to clarify morality in a logical (not empirical) manner that showed that moral conduct is the product of an understanding of scripture and a relationship with the holy spirit. Accordingly he asserts that truth, as revealed in scripture requires two factors to be understood: Diligence and piety. "on one hand, we must have knowledge to find truth, and on the other hand we must deserve to get the knowledge." Let's map this out in a logical sequence and see what it looks like.

1. You must have knowledge to find truth
2. You must deserve to get the knowledge

The knowledge that he speaks of is the knowledge of scripture. The truth he speaks about is the truth about the nature of God and the revelation of Jesus Christ as God's son. In St. Augustine's time only a privileged few people were ever able to read scripture. Knowledge was considered a blessing from God. Truth could only be achieved after being righteous, pious and diligent in the reading of scripture and in prayer. His version of morality required an external source of enlightenment, and a standard to live by. There was no accounting for the internal workings of the mind.

Furthermore, he asserted that in order to understand scripture one would employ reason *and* authority.

In Section 3 of his treatise he states that what we learn comes to us through reasoning and authority because reason without authority is weak. He attempts to explain that those who criticize scripture cannot be reasoned with, as they start out by making argument. (How can authority work when it is questioned?) In such a conflict, where the attack comes from outside the structure of the church, the authority of church leaders and scripture itself carries no weight and reason would then be left to stand alone, making it weak.

St. Augustine's text was intended to identify the strategies used by Manicheans (Gnostics) who were thought to be subverting Christianity for their own purposes. He accused the Manicheans of finding fault with Holy Scripture and trying to show Christians that they were chaste when they were not. I have often wondered how St. Augustine knew the Manicheans were not chaste.

If you are to become virtuous, you must submit to God and scripture and work diligently at it, a common theme in current Christian teachings. St. Augustine clearly asserted that a Christian man's definition of what-is-moral comes from a supernatural source that is both outside of man and inside of man. This occurs through communion with God via the Holy Spirit and human soul as described in sections 22 and 23 of his treatise.

It is my humble opinion that St. Augustine had it all wrong. The myths found in scripture attempt to tell stories with moral lessons and nothing more. His conflict with the Manicheans was actually a race between two cultures who attempted to popularize their own versions of history. Even still, some of those stories from the Gnostics or the Christians are not good examples of morality at all.

St. Augustine's assertion is in direct conflict with both modern secular philosophy and neurological evidence from a number of studies that show neurons firing within and between their various structures of the brain when making all kinds of decisions, including moral ones.

I won't be so foolish as to say that a brain scan proves there is no soul, nor will I assert that brain scans prove there is no interaction between God and man. Instead I will simply say that there is no physical evidence of what St. Augustine asserts what-so-ever. Carl Sagan's "dragon in the garage" comes to mind.

St. Augustine's idea that diligence, piety and communion with the Holy Spirit will create a moral mankind was nothing more than wild eyed speculation.

In all fairness I probably would not have done any better had I been born sixteen hundred years ago. It would be different if he were to make this assertion today.

(23)

Disappointment

It was a deeply disappointing day—Nov 30th 2007—Jeff Olsson

The Catholic Church's attack on the morality of others continues, 1600 years later, in the latest encyclical letter from Pope Benedict XVI entitled Spe Salvi (Which means "Saved by Hope" in Latin), November 30th 2007.

To the Pope, secular morality is seen as a means of rationalizing why we live in such an unjust world. The Pope asserts that it leads to atrocity. I have clarified and converted section 42 of the encyclical into bullet form:

1. Moral atheism is derived from a protest against perceived injustices in the world
2. Moral atheism contests God because he is seen to be neither good nor just (ie. God is not great)
3. Atheists feel that it is for the sake of morality that God must be contested
4. Atheists think that since God does not exist man must establish his own form of justice
5. It is false and presumptuous to think man can achieve justice without God

6. It is no accident that this idea has lead to the greatest forms of cruelty and injustice
7. A world that creates its own justice is a world without hope.

My comments: I suspect that the Pope is using St. Paul's definition of an atheist, (atheoi) which means that any non Christian is an atheist. I also suspect that he presumes that all other religions are man made where Christianity was created through divine intervention.

I challenge the Pope to explain how it is that humankind's attempts at imposing justice, secular or not, are any worse than that imposed by the God of the Old Testament who is said to have obliterated entire cities with fire storms, brought disease, pestilence and war in order to punish "injustice" in the world.

I find it absolutely reprehensible that the Pope blames unbelief in Christ for the troubles of the world.

There are also some pretty serious problems with the Popes version of morality, and the primary one is that it leads to inflexible and dogmatic thinking, especially where the use of scripture is seen as 'most important' in making moral decisions. Dogmatism is often defined as a doctrine or a body of doctrines relating to matters such as morality and faith, set forth in an authoritative manner by a church.

When people attempt to protect what they believe to be true and their perception defies rational thought or clear physical evidence to the contrary, it is likely that they are practicing a form of dogmatic thinking.

It is my firm assertion that the pope is being quite dogmatic when he asserts that atheism leads to cruelty and injustice. Especially when experience and research shows that non-Christians are fully capable of being moral, ethical and caring. You must ignore the greater portions of modern history to come to the conclusion that science and secularism have resulted have resulted in the most horrific forms of cruelty and injustice.

What about the great advances in science that have prevented billions of deaths by the creation of hearty drought resistant crops, potable water systems, sanitation systems? What about a disease like small pox that has been eradicated, after 300-500 million people were estimated to have died from it? What about the dramatic increase in average lifespan in western countries where secular solutions have been used in various government, medical communities, food distribution services, transportation and communication services etc? What secular atrocities could even come close undoing the sheer magnitude of these numbers?

The idea that people without God cannot be as moral as Christians or that any one religion owns morality is patently false. Were it not for the assumption that Christian theology, thinking and morality are superior to all others, the pope would not be able to make such an assertion in the first place. It's arrogant.

(24)

The Encyclopedias

I will never forget the day that our first set of encyclopedias arrived at our home. I was only about 7 years old. They arrived in compact, heavy boxes that needed careful unpacking. My father took each book out and examined it front and back to ensure that it was not damaged. He wiped away the packing dust with his big hands as he placed the books neatly into a pile on the hardwood floor. Once satisfied that each book had arrived undamaged, he carefully placed each book on our book shelf.

It was obvious that these books were important to my father. I was cautioned to "be careful" many times when reading them. A genuine sense of awe overcame me whenever I read about far off lands or planets or different cultures. The encyclopedias Americana, Canadiana and Britannica, seemed like the sum total of all human knowledge to me at the time. Our bookshelf was 10 feet wide and these encyclopedias took up much of it leaving only a small amount of room for my mother's knick knacks.

Our family lived in a remote village named Gillam, about 650 kilometers north of the American border by air. The population of Gillam was about 1500 at the time, and there was no road connecting it to any other villages. The only way in or out of Gillam was by train, or by aircraft. The school went up to grade ten, and if you wanted more education you had to move to Thompson, the nearest city that was 300 kilometers away.

Such was my life! I lived in a small town where my world view was shaped by what I learned in school, what I watched on CBC and a wonderfully large set of encyclopedias. (CBC was the only TV channel that was broadcast in Gillam at the time)

I loved those books, they had answers to questions about everything I could possibly imagine. I would walk in the forest and when a question arose about a bug or a tree, or a frog, I would run home and look it up in those books. Very seldom did they fail me. We did not attend any church and my parents never talked about God unless I asked a specific question about religion. My life was basically a-theistic, I lived without God.

Five years later, after some marital turmoil and a visit by the local Anglican priest our family started attending church. My father, mother and I had deeply religious experiences which came out of our participation in the charismatic renewal movement and we became quite sure that we had found God in a very genuine way. In grade eleven I was enrolled in a private Christian school in Selkirk, near Winnipeg.

During one of his trips to Winnipeg to visit me at school, my father took me to Hull's book store to buy me my very own leather bound copy of the Bible. He said, "This book has everything in it that a person needs to get through life." He told me it was "the owners manual for the human body."

It was a lot smaller than the encyclopedias.

Something had changed inside of us and the encyclopedias began to gather dust.

In the years that followed I met and married my wonderful wife Leslie and I began to attended ministry training to prepare for the priesthood. I was eventually ordained and appointed rector of the same small parish my family had had its conversion experience in. Life was good for me then, I felt I had the answers I needed.

Years later when I began to doubt and raise questions about the Christian faith I faced dogmatic thinking head on. I was appalled at the manner in which homosexuals were dismissed by Church leaders and parishioners alike. I was also amazed by the believers' ability to ignore the pain of others who had been so seriously damaged by the residential school system, a system administered in large part by the Anglican Church.

Since I was now the one who raised questions about the validity of Christian thinking on these matters I was admonished for it by some of the parishioners. Dogmatism was rampant, bible verses were quoted 'ad nauseum' by those who needed justification to discriminate against others. What's worse, much of the scripture that they quoted was used within its correct context, theologically speaking.

(25)

A Brief Glimpse at Evolution

"All evolution in thought and conduct must at first appear as heresy and misconduct."—George Bernard Shaw quotes (Irish literary Critic, Playwright and Essayist. 1925 Nobel Prize for Literature, 1856-1950)

It was a beautiful summer day when my nephew Nathan came to visit us. We decided to go for a walk in the city. As we meandered down Broadway the traffic was thick and noisy. The smell of hot dog and chip vendors hung in the air. The noise of people walking, standing, chatting and laughing on the sidewalk drowned out our own conversation. The city of Winnipeg was alive.

In the large median section between the east and west bound lanes there are elm trees that make wonderful shade from the sun. Park benches, concrete, bricks, grass and a fountain adorn the median. We stopped for a break and as we sat on the grass near one of the elm trees and it was not long before Nate found some ants crawling around the base of a tree. In the midst of the noise and traffic we observed them and noticed a 'battle' going on between at least two different species of ants and some rather unfortunate forest tent caterpillars, an invasive species that drops from the tree on a long strand of silk.

Teams of the small black ants would attack the caterpillars and cart them off as they twisted at their lanky bodies. Larger carpenter (?) ants would attack the caterpillars in a similar way and cart them off in pieces. There were ant and caterpillar parts everywhere.

Nate show great curiosity regarding these ants and during our discussion he asked "whose tree is this" do the big ones own it or do the little ones own it? It was then that I saw the curiosity in his eyes that I realized how important curiosity is.

Why are they fighting Unc'a Jeff? I answered him, and for about five minutes I explained about black ants, carpenter ants, caterpillars, scent trails, territory and the struggle for survival faced by each species. Nathan showed great interest, it was all very important to him. He understood that there was much more to learn. (so did I)

Later, as the two of us walked home in silence I thought, "When did I lose my curiosity?" How did that small book called the bible ever become more important than the encyclopedic volumes of data that tell us in a very accurate way who we are, how we evolved and what the world is? How could I have ever thought it was immoral to question my faith, or to wonder? Why was my own curiosity so obscured by the idea that 'God did it'?

I have since rekindled my love for the encyclopedias that my father unpacked so many years ago; I have regained the sense of awe that I once felt when I read about far off lands and the amazing findings of science. I can walk in the forest and see life teeming around me. I can respect other cultures for what they are without the need to diminish their beauty. I can see that other people have developed the same way that we did, only in different environments.

I can also see how we are hurting each other because of our beliefs about things that no one has ever been able to prove.

To me, there is something right about this new way of looking at things.

Evolution

The way evolution by natural selection works is rather interesting. First an animal is born; let's say it's a gazelle. If it survives long enough to mate its genes are passed along. But if it is slower than other gazelles, or perhaps it has poorer eyesight or is harder of hearing, it will lose the race when a predator gives chase. This race between predator and prey happens very often and the herd is forced to give up the animals that have the poorest senses, or are slow. Often, only the fast animals with bright senses survive long enough to mate and bear young. And so the population is shaped, one gazelle at a time, by this selective factor. It is not a game of chance; there is a direct pressure to ensure that the survivors are the faster, brighter animals. As a result, gazelles are very fast, can see for long distances and can hear quite well.

On the other hand the predators, let's say lions, need to be fast too. They need to work together to hunt gazelle, to communicate via body language and vocalizations and to read each others actions in order to corner and catch their prey. A relatively weak male lion may be able to participate in the catch from a hunt that was successful since female lions do the bulk of the hunting and share their catch with the pride. A weaker younger lion may survive well beyond its age of maturation and live to be old enough to mate. Unless it can find an available mate it will never get to pass along its genes.

Younger male lions are often driven out of the pride by larger older lions, while females usually remain with one pride for life. Consequently, the smaller weaker lion is forced to leave and will go out into the savannah to seek out any female that is available from another pride. Unless he can find an older lion that he can beat in order to mate with his females or find a stray female, he may never get to mate. Without the cooperative environment that comes with his home pride, and especially if he is a poor hunter, he may starve to death alone in the savannah. And so it is that populations of lions are shaped by selective forces that separate out the weak and less able, one at a time.

It is important to note how cruel this natural process is. If a gazelle is born a slow runner because of inferior genes, it will have its throat ripped out and its body torn apart as it is eaten by a predator. There is no justice for those gazelles that are slow, there is no way for them to seek asylum. Countless gazelles die in order for genetic diversity to play its role in this process, where only the fastest gazelles with the brightest senses are left to live on.

If you were to observe a pride of lions you would quickly see how sociable and cooperative each individual is. You would also remark at how cruel such a lonely starvation would be to an outcast animal that was born with the faculty to be so sociable. This process goes on every day, even as you read this letter.

The process that made us into the humans we are today was virtually the same, except that some of the latest attributes that natural selection produced included an advantageous brain to body mass ratio. It also included the ability to communicate complicated ideas and to cooperate for hunting, the ability to perform higher thinking and foresee long term consequences which has allowed us to shape our own behaviour and has given us greater adaptability in adverse environments. As millennia passed, those who could not perform these functions lost the competitions for food and shelter. They suffered a similar cruel end just like the animals I mentioned earlier.

Charles Darwin was a keen observer of nature. He did well to explain how the process of evolution works, it is good science. And yet he was attacked incessantly by those who would not hear the truth. He was attacked by those who could not allow themselves to believe that earth's inhabitants evolved by naturalistic processes; they insisted that supernatural influence was involved at every step.

In a letter to his close friend Asa Gray, a botanist who defended his theory in America on May 18th 1860 Darwin remarked that the attacks against him and his theory were mounting. Had it not been for those few men who pressed forward with his theory in the halls of the universities his theory would have been a mere "flash in the pan".

Which explanation would best tell how life as we know it came to be? Debates raged on as more and more professors took up Darwin's torch. They used logic and good science to show that naturalistic processes were all that was needed for life to evolve into what it is today.

The battle lines were drawn in the great halls of the universities in England, Canada and in the United States, academia was at war with itself as a reformation occurred. As the processes that framed Darwin's ideas about evolution were clearly explained, more and more people began to see how it could be true, how the world had come to be as it is without the need for intervention from the supernatural.

Darwin and other scientists looked deeper into the "how" of biological life and found things that both amazed them and repulsed them. In many cases their own beliefs were changed by what they saw. Having said this I must point out that those who portray Darwin as the author of an atheistic world view misunderstood him completely. In another letter to Asa Gray, four days later, on May 22nd 1860 Darwin remarked that he had no intentions of writing "atheistically", but admitted that he could not see the evidence of God's beneficence as other people seem too. (By the way I highly recommend that you read Darwin's letter from the link above or in the references section of this book.)

And so it was that Darwin not only saw that nature came to be 'as it is' by the process of evolution, he also saw that there was still room for belief in a higher power which he described as a designer of natural laws. He was repulsed by the idea that a loving God would create the Ichneumonidæ fly that lays its eggs in the belly of a caterpillar (causing unimaginable suffering to the caterpillar as the eggs develop into larvae), and yet he admitted that laws were quite possibly designed by an omniscient higher power, laws that blindly guided the process of evolution.

What Darwin had observed and reported (and what his opponents were railing against) was that God did not appear to be directly involved in the process itself. To Darwin, God appeared to have set the wheels of evolution in motion and let them spin according to the laws of nature. To me it seems that Darwin's "problem" was that God did not seem terribly concerned about the resulting cruelty.

If I was to accept that evolution is a fact and simultaneously make the claim that God's existence is also a fact, I am left with the question of how an omnipotent, omniscient, benevolent God could let this cruel process continue. Either God uses this process and approves of the cruelty on a daily basis *or* God doesn't care about the suffering inherent in natural selection *or* God is powerless to stop it. Sounds Epicurean doesn't it? Well it is.

> "Is God willing to prevent evil, but not able? Then he is not omnipotent.
>
> Is he able, but not willing? Then he is malevolent.
>
> Is he both able and willing? Then where does evil come from?
>
> Is he neither able nor willing? Then why call him God?"
>
> —Epicurus (BC 341-270)

When I left the church, I was similarly upset with God's apparent lack of action. God did not seem to care one lick about what happened to thousands of residential school students hurt by his holy institution. One look at their damaged lives tells the story. Nor does he seem to care much about homosexuals who are being demonized by the conservative church.

Evolution is not a philosophy, but instead a physical reality. In 1543 Rheticus published Copernicus's work showing that heliocentrism was logical and mathematically defensible. The sun was shown to be centre of our solar system, a physical fact, not a philosophy. By default this finding showed that the geocentric, bible based philosophies about mankind's importance in this universe were without any backing in the physical realm. The religious world was quite upset.

Likewise, many biblical stories and religious philosophies are proven inaccurate or completely false because of the new understanding of physical reality that has emerged from the evolutionary sciences. Again, this does not mean that evolution is in itself a philosophy. Evolution is nothing more than an empirical fact proven out through countless hours of research by scientists, numerous pieces of evidence found by archeologists, laboratory analysis of DNA evidence, biological science, chemistry, physics and much more.

Just before I left the church I came to a fuller understanding of how evolution works when I read a book called The Selfish Gene, written by Richard Dawkins. It helped me to see how the physical processes of evolution occur at the individual level. We are the result of DNA molecules that have copied themselves over and over again for many millennia.

Our diversity and the inevitable movement towards biological complexity are a result of a combination of various errors in the copying process coupled with natural selection, in diverse species. We are a lowly creature that carries a replicating molecule around within each of the cells of our body. DNA molecules were not made *for* us; we are a *result* of them. (A physical reality). While my body is still relatively young, it is my genes that are ancient; they carry the digital legacy of my ancestors dating back millions of years. This is not a philosophy, even though it sounds like it. It is instead a verifiable fact that has forced me to rethink my assumptions about who I am, how I came to be and to reconsider my belief in a creator.

There are little strands of DNA,

it took me forty years to see,

that we can't say that *we* own *them*

because *they* created you and me.

> They copy and they copy,
>
> in our microscopes we see,
>
> and still some say that *we* own them;
>
> ... they ignore reality.
>
> —jo

Rethink Darwin

Take all of your preconceptions about Darwin, especially those taught by the religious right, and cast them aside. History shows us that Darwin attended church every Sunday until *after* his daughter Annie died in 1851, only then did he lose his faith in a benevolent God. Even still, he participated in church events and fundraisers; he would walk his wife Emma to the gate of the church where she would attend each Sunday service. While she was in church he would go for a walk in the countryside.

Darwin was a man who dared to think, a keen observer who worried about the consequences of what he observed. Proof of his concern can be found in his letter to Asa Gray, one of the chief American defenders of his thesis where he stated *"all these laws may have been expressly designed by an omniscient Creator, who foresaw every future event & consequence"*. From this we see that Darwin proclaimed his faith in a creator God (as it was) to the very man that was defending his theory of evolution in American universities nine years after the death of his daughter.

This is not the Charles Darwin that is portrayed by the religious right. This was a reasonable man. A man who dared to think when faced with facts, rather than duck under the safety of a dogmatic system of belief.

Darwin never did become an atheist like me. There are many people, including myself, who do not consider atheism a natural outcome of belief in evolution. If you look closely you can easily see the reasonableness of Darwin's observations about evolution.

(25)

Anglicanism and Homosexuality

"So far as I can tell there is not one word in the Gospels in praise of intelligence."—Lord Bertrand Russell (1872-1970), British Nobel Laureate, mathematician, philosopher and peace activist

For Anglican homosexuals, living a full life within the church is problematic, especially when the church loves its creeds more than it loves you.

The Anglican Church of Canada has struggled with the issue of homosexuality as a valid lifestyle for those within its ranks since the early nineteen seventies. If you were to say that all of the debate has been 'open' it would be an understatement and if you were to say that the debate has been polite it would be a gross exaggeration. In all fairness most Anglicans (including homosexuals), are polite and friendly people who wish not to offend anyone. The problem is that homosexual Anglicans have not felt acceptance for who they are by their conservative counterparts. They are politely told that they are sinners and the implication expressed to them is that God will abandon them to hell because of their homosexual lifestyle. In all fairness to conservative Anglicans they have not really chastised anyone for merely having same sex attraction, more than to say it is classed as a sinful thought. It is the *act* of homosexual sex that is seen as a distinct problem as it is seen as open rebellion against the "good teachings" provided in scripture.

If you do not believe me, please read on.

The Anglican Church, being what it is, is a community where the recitation of creeds is the order of the day. If you were to pop into an Anglican church on a Sunday morning you would be in contact with people who *like* to recite these creeds. They take *comfort* in the creeds. Anglicans who prefer this type of worship will tell you so. Many will tell you *why* they like it this way. Even though they are small in number in some communities, there are two things that you need to remember about devout (modern) Anglicans:

1. They choose to go church, in a society where church going is not so popular any more, and
2. They generally prefer a liturgical church service to the guitar slinging clappy clap services that have become the norm in other denominations.

Humour me for a moment and imagine a group of people who gather weekly into small parishes across Canada. They gather together for the purpose of repeating words from a book, out loud and in a worshipful manner. They kneel at certain times during the liturgy; they bow at the altar after communion. They also sing some very beautiful hymns and listen to a homily each week. Some make the sign of the cross as they pray. These special words, the words that they repeat weekly are not just random words but specific words that they have come to believe are true. The words hold deep meaning to them. These are words that they feel make them who they are. These words make them distinct from others in the world. They are Anglicans.

Now imagine that you were to arbitrarily change the words in the books. People will notice the change, some will react. For some the change is too much and they begin to complain. Come back 15 or 20 years later and some of them are still complaining about the change in the words in the book. They are Anglicans.

Is it so hard to imagine that there would be some pretty serious debate before anyone would be allowed to change a single jot or tittle at all in those books?

In reality, this is how it has been since 1549 when the first version of the Anglican Book Of Common Prayer was written after the English reformation. Another revision was written in 1552 that brought the book further away from its Catholic counterpart, but it was not published until 1559 due to an excursion back into Catholicism by Mary I. The next revision was published in 1662 after the English Civil War and that book has remained as the Common Book of Prayer in England since then. Over 300 years have passed. In Canada the 1662 version of the book was modified only slightly in 1918, and made more Canadian again in 1962. The same book (essentially) was used for three hundred years before it was Canadianized.

The *preface* of the 1962 version of the Book of Common Prayer (Canadian version) States that it has been "three hundred years" since any changes have been made to the book. It also states that the book is a 'priceless' possession of the Church. This was a book that was not meant to be altered without deep consideration.

Now, (surprise of all surprises), imagine that the change that I am referring to is to add or remove words necessary to allow for the acceptance of homosexuals into full communion within the Anglican Church, *and* to allow them to marry one another.

Gaining acceptance of homosexuality is not going to be an easy battle to win within an orthodox Christian sect. Sure, some of the people that recite the Anglican creeds have no problem with homosexuality what-so-ever, especially in the larger urban centers where a more liberal interpretation of scripture seems to be the norm. But for those folks that hold fast to the ancient ways, for those that like their creeds and books and bibles just the way they are, there is going to be a debate, and even a fight. And it is going to last for a long time. A very long time.

Anglicans of the 1970's probably watched the evening news and likely knew that homosexuality was no longer considered a psychological disorder in Canada or the USA. (It was removed from the Diagnostics and Statistics Manual used by Psychologists and Psychiatrists in 1973 and this fact made the national news a number of times.) They probably watched as CBC news asked Canadians on the street what they thought about the issue and were shocked, or surprised at how some folks had no problem with homosexuality at all. They probably had heard that the Canadian Human Rights Commission was seeking legislative change in order to protect homosexuals from discrimination. They knew that society was changing and that homosexuality in Canada was beginning to be tolerated. And so the Bishops of the Anglican Church, facing internal pressure to accept homosexuality from parishes in urban centers created a task force to discuss this issue and seek a course of action for Canadian Anglicans.

On Friday, *Feb. 3, 1978* the Anglican News Service reported that a "highly emotional" discussion and debate on the rights of homosexuals had become divisive. The House of Bishops was commissioning a task force to help deal with the deliberations.

This Anglican News Service article included a reprint of the *press release* by the Anglican Church that stated that while homosexuals are entitled to equal protection under the law, that only sexual unions of male and female can form the covenant of "Holy Matrimony". They recognized that some homosexuals form relationships that are of comfort to them but that these relationships are not to be confused with marriage. They went on to say that the church should not do anything that appears to support any assertion that gay marriage is acceptable. No matter how nicely the press release was worded, it still meant that homosexuals were not included into the life of the church.

In 1978, the Anglican Church of Canada formally began a debate on the validity of same sex marriage. Bishops knew full well that the inclusion of homosexuals would mean that the Church would be forced to split, as dissenters would not tolerate such a change. They also knew that full rejection would mean that the church would be forced to split as those hoping for change would grow impatient. Instead the Bishops commissioned a task force and subsequent studies. As a result the debate has raged on for over thirty years and has stifled the full inclusion of homosexuals in parishes that would otherwise have no problem with their inclusion, except that they would lose communion with the rest of the church. The Anglican Journal, an award winning Canadian Anglican newspaper has (at times) had more letters to the editor about homosexuality in the church than other pressing issues like the resolution of the residential schools abuses. The letters to the editor on this topic have been so numerous that people have written letters to complain *about* the number of letters to the editor.

People were upset and the debate continued . . .

In 1992 James Ferry, a priest in the diocese of Toronto was stripped of his licence and was prevented from functioning as a priest after a Bishops Court decision found him guilty of cohabiting with another man. His living arrangements were discovered by a parishioner who somehow "infiltrated" his residence and saw the two men living together. The parishioner reported Ferry to the Bishop of Toronto. Ferry left the Anglican Church. Six years later, after considerable flack from parishes in Toronto he was eventually given a partial reinstatement. While he now works at the Metropolitan Community Church of Toronto, a United Church, he occasionally celebrates Eucharist at the Church of the Holy Trinity in Toronto. In an odd turn of events Archbishop Terence Finlay, the Bishop who found Ferry guilty and dismissed him was recently charged and disciplined by his own successor (as Bishop of Toronto) for assisting in a same sex marriage. Who'd figure?

The contradictions are astounding.

In June 1994 a meeting of 700 like minded Anglicans, forming the Anglican Essentials Movement occurred in Montreal. The event was sponsored by Anglican Renewal Ministries, Barnabus Anglican Ministries and the Prayer Book Society of Canada. This group produced and affirmed a document called The Montreal Declaration in which the orthodox theological roots of the church were discussed at length. This inspired the subsequent formation of the Essentials Council, now called the Anglican Federation, a group around which orthodox believers rally.

The Montreal Declaration states: *"Together we reaffirm the Anglican Christianity that finds expression in the historic standards of the ecumenical creeds, the Thirty-Nine Articles, the Solemn Declaration of 1893, and the 1962 Book of Common Prayer."*

The Montreal Declaration also states:

> *"14. The Standards of Sexual Conduct God designed human sexuality not only for procreation but also for the joyful expression of love, honour, and fidelity between wife and husband. These are the only sexual relations that biblical theology deems good and holy. Adultery, fornication, and homosexual unions are intimacies contrary to God's design. The church must seek to minister healing and wholeness to those who are sexually scarred, or who struggle with ongoing sexual temptations, as most people do. Homophobia and all forms of sexual hypocrisy and abuse are evils against which Christians must ever be on their guard. The church may not lower God's standards of sexual morality for any of its members, but must honour God by upholding these standards tenaciously in face of society's departures from them. Congregations must seek to meet the particular needs for friendship and community that single persons have. (Genesis 1:26-28; 2:21-24; Matthew 5:27-32; 19:3-12; Luke 7:36-50; John*

8:1-11; Romans 1:21-28; 3:22-24; 1 Corinthians 6:9-11, 13-16; 7:7; Ephesians 5:3; 1 Timothy 1:8-11; 3:2-4, 12.)"

A Response to The Montreal Declaration and its statement about Human Sexuality (Section 14).

While I am deeply disturbed by this entire section of the declaration, I would like to draw your attention to one line of text that seems particularly hypocritical: *"Homophobia and all forms of sexual hypocrisy and abuse are evils against which Christians must ever be on their guard."* How can it be that they say they are concerned about homophobia while they are quoting biblical passages that condemn the individual who is a homosexual?

The Montreal Declaration asserts that unrepentant homosexuals are going to hell, "1 Corinthians 6:9-11 states: *9 Or do you not know that the unrighteous will not inherit the kingdom of God? Do not be deceived; neither fornicators, nor idolaters, nor adulterers, nor effeminate, nor homosexuals, 10 nor thieves, nor the covetous, nor drunkards, nor revilers, nor swindlers, will inherit the kingdom of God. 11 Such were some of you; but you were washed, but you were sanctified, but you were justified in the name of the Lord Jesus Christ and in the Spirit of our God."*

The Montreal Declaration asserts that homosexuals are criminal, "1 Timothy 1:8-11 states: *8 But we know that the Law is good, if one uses it lawfully, 9 realizing the fact that law is not made for a righteous person, but for those who are lawless and rebellious, for the ungodly and sinners, for the unholy and profane, for those who kill their fathers or mothers, for murderers 10 and immoral men and homosexuals and kidnappers and liars and perjurers, and whatever else is contrary to sound teaching, 11 according to the glorious gospel of the blessed God, with which I have been entrusted."*

The model of human sexuality presented in the The Montreal Declaration is cynical in nature and betrays an ignorance of modern science on the part of those who have affirmed the declaration. Had this model been contrived today we would forced to ignore substantial evidence contrary to its assertions in order to accept it as plausible. It is more akin to hate speech than a compassionate description of homosexual behaviour. And yet people still accept section 14 as true because the underlying statements come from scripture.

The problem with 1 Corinthians 6:9-11 and 1 Timothy 1:8-11, two of the scriptures used as the foundation for section 14, is that St. Paul puts homosexuality in the same classification as a crime when in it is not one. (Neither is effeminate behaviour) This is not just an opinion, but is shown through empirical studies of a variety of species including humans. Simply put, homosexual behaviour occurs naturally and without harm to populations or to the individuals involved.

Those who dispute the validity of homosexuality often confuse the existence of same sex attraction and the resultant coupling with the cause of same sex attraction. They say it is a choice. While the physiological cause of homosexual attraction is currently a topic of research and debate among scientists there can be no doubt about the fact that over fifteen hundred species of animals, humans among them, have been observed to exhibit homosexual tendencies. Over four hundred of those species have been studied extensively and there is no documented evidence that homosexual behaviour causes harm to the larger population or the individuals involved. St. Paul's assertion that it is a crime is unfounded and slanderous.

The fields of psychology, neurology, ethology (of humans and animals), biology and sociology all bring forth reams of evidence that point to a model of human operation that is both humbling and compelling when compared with the ideas presented in section 14 of The Montreal Declaration. Humans are amazingly diverse and have an enormous capacity for kindness. The bulk of humans (homosexuals included) are well behaved and sociable. No amount of research can find evidence that shows statistically significant differences in crime rates for homosexuals than that observed for heterosexuals. There are other causes for criminal behaviour that are well known in the social sciences and criminology.

While long term mate bonding may occur at a lower rate in homosexual humans there is no indication of this in animal populations, leading one to speculate that the problem is associated with societal acceptance of homosexual individuals and lack of societal support for homosexual couples.

There is also compelling evidence that shows the brains of homosexuals are actually structured like those of the opposite sex. Evidence that homosexuality may be caused by conditions in the womb prior to birth has been known about for over 2 years and has been observed in other species than humans.

In summary, to compare homosexuality to criminal behaviour is to ignore good science. To marginalize homosexuals because of ideas codified in an Iron Age text written by a tent maker from the Middle East betrays your incorrigible nature. There is room in your church for a belief in God and an acceptance of science and homosexuals. You have no need to marginalize anyone because of your belief in scripture.

For further information see: *Gay brains structured like those of the opposite sex*, *Womb environment 'makes men gay*, *Gay animals out of the closet?* and *The Natural "Crime Against Nature" A Brief Survey of Homosexual Behaviors In Animals*

The events in the church have continued to unfold. In 2002, the Diocese of New Westminster voted to allow same sex marriage, in a process that included representatives from each parish. As a result some Canadian parishes have threatened to leave the Anglican Communion and other Canadian parishes have sought Episcopal oversight from conservative Anglican Bishops on other continents. National churches in Uganda and Nigeria have declared that they will no longer remain in communion with the Anglican Church of Canada unless reparations are made in the Diocese of New Westminster. They expect discipline to occur, and want dissident liberals removed from their posts.

In 2004, after 26 years of commissions and debate, synods and votes, yet another theological commission was assigned the task of determining if same sex marriage is a matter of doctrine or and issue that can be settled by individual bishops at their discretion. The Commission found that same sex marriage is a matter of doctrine in the same sense that salvation is. While it is not a core doctrine it will still require a change to the canons of the church, which means that a two thirds vote is required for a change to take place. More study will take place and a report will be tabled in 2010 at the next General Synod.

After 32 years of debate Anglicans are finally going to look and see how Christian doctrine will affect this issue. I honestly thought they *had* been arguing about doctrine all this time. It took almost 300 years before changes were initiated to create the 'modern' 1962 version of the Book of Common Prayer. How long will it be before Anglicans embrace the doctrinal changes necessary to end the conservative bigotry practiced by some of those who stand behind their pulpits, and their supporters in the pews.

In 2007, the Diocese of Ottawa, Montreal, and Huron vote to accept same sex marriage.

August 3 2008, Anglican Journal, Bishops from all over the world meeting in Canterbury England agree that a moratorium on same sex marriage will ensure the unity of the church Those who threaten to break communion if homosexuality is accepted within the Anglican Communion should be ashamed of themselves. It is time to call their bluff and let them go.

(26)

Honest Doubt

"Aristotle maintained that women have fewer teeth than men; although he was twice married, it never occurred to him to verify this statement by examining his wives' mouths."—Bertrand Russell (1872-1970)

I remember it like it was yesterday (maybe it was.). It was a beautiful summer morning, the birds were singing and the air smelled like spring lilacs. Leslie and I were heading to work in our little Honda Civic, the windows were open, the wind was blowing in what little hair I have left, and the engine of my Honda was purring in my one good ear.

Winnipeg "prairie" summers are the best in Canada.

Then I saw a red light out of my good eye.

I turned on the radio to listen to Wheeler and Hal on Power 97, our favorite morning radio show. Wheeler and Hal are two very funny individuals who do a comedy piece about Hal's heart talking to him after eating too many hamburgers, "Ohhhhhh Nooooooo" Hal's heart groaned as he gobbled down more burgers. We laugh out loud.

Green light

The station cued up a couple of songs, AC/DC—Hells Bells, followed by Puddle of Mud—Schizophrenic Psycho

Red Light

Schizophrenic psycho is just ending and a strange voice comes on the air, "Excuse me I would like to interrupt for a moment . . ." an evangelist preacher from Calvary Temple Church begins to do just what he said he was going to do. He interrupts my pleasant thoughts and pitches *his* version of "Jesus" to me. He tells me that doubt is ok as long as it is "a stepping stone to faith". As a former Christian I find his message strange and annoying. It's only been 5 years since I have resigned my holy orders with the Anglican Church of Canada, and you'd think I would still get it, but I don't. I was tempted to turn the radio off again but thought that I'd listen to his whole message this time, "lets see what he has to say", I thought.

You can hear it for yourself here:
http://www.ctwinnipeg.com/files/CalvaryTemple-Doubt.mp3

I thought about what he had to say for a moment, It was honest doubt that got me where I am, and honest doubt gave me a chance to look seriously at questions like:

Why did doubting Thomas get to see Jesus, scars and all, when all we get is an admonishment by a cheesy pastor to "just believe" in the face of some pretty serious doubts? The fact that the average person cannot access this type of "special revelation" makes the story smack of dishonest fabrication.

Why am I told that my doubts are not "honest" when the conclusion of my investigation (thus far) is that there were no supernatural events surrounding the life of Jesus? I have not seen any revelation what-so-ever, when I have spent almost 30 years of my life looking for that revelation. I am now one of those many people who do not believe Jesus was a supernatural being that walked on water or rose from the dead.

Why am I told that I am "unwilling" to know the truth? I was quite willing. After 30 years I must conclude that it is God who is a "no show". Have you ever read the Jefferson Bible Bruce? You should!

A couple more thoughts crossed my mind:

1. Bruce Martin thinks that he has found the truth and that all others who disagree are wrong, even when they have strong arguments against him.
2. He makes a claim of special revelation, but once you look into it, you see that he is only quoting scripture. He has never seen God, or Jesus, or an Angel, or the Devil for that matter.

3. He assumes that we'd simply rather not know when there are millions of us who have investigated his religion for ourselves and have found that his position lacks satisfying evidence.
4. Not only does it lack evidence, it is logically indefensible. He only has emotion to run on.

Green Light

I asked Leslie, "Did I *EVER* sound like that when I was a preacher? This guy is manipulative."

Fearing a negative response I began to mount a mental defense before she answered

"Not at all", she answered, "but you were enthusiastic about your faith". I cannot deny that. "But . . . did I ever intrude into peoples lives like this guy; I don't remember pulling guilt trips, I mean, why would he think to tell this stuff to people who are not interested, he accuses those who are not interested of being unwilling to know the truth?"

Before she answered I remembered the times I had officiated at numerous funerals, weddings, and Remembrance Day services, where I always said a few words in an attempt to show the relevance of faith. "Jeff, you told people *about* your faith, but you did your evangelizing one on one and always with people who were interested. They came to you". I remembered a few of the many times I had shared my faith and commented, "They always asked first, I just don't remember shoving anything down anyone's throat."

Perhaps I did do some shoving but just cannot remember, or wasn't aware. Leslie countered "But this guy is no more intrusive than the guy who sells beds from Best Sleep Centre, Jeff, it's just a commercial".

I considered her words for a moment "Yeah, but it's a fucking annoying commercial", "Yes it is", she replied.

Red light

The conversation subsided and the remainder of the trip was spent listening to the radio and laughing along with two very funny comedians. Green Light

(27)

Hope

In the morning of August 24, 79 CE a loud roar tore across the skies of Pompeii. Pliney the Younger had heard thunder before but he had never heard anything like *this*. A large black cloud of gasses, molten rock and fire rose up above the mountain of the god Hercules.

When the rock and ash began to rain down on the village the roofs of many houses were crushed and many people were killed, some instantly. There was little or no time to run, since the plume from the eruption of Mount Vesuvius extended for many miles. Pliney's mother begged him to escape as best he could. He was one of the lucky ones who made it far enough away; his written record of the unfolding of the disaster is still with us today:

> "Ashes were already falling, but not yet thickly . . . When night fell, not one such as when there is no moon or the sky is cloudy, but a night like being in a closed place with the lights out. One could hear the wailing of women, the crying of children, the shouting of men; they called each other, some their parents, others their children, still others their mates, trying to recognize each other by their voices. Some lamented their own fate, others the fate of their loved ones. There were even those who out of their fear of death prayed for death"

On that fateful day in 79 CE all hope was lost. While estimates vary, it is generally thought that 38 percent of Pompeii's citizens died that day. Many of them suffered excruciating pain from burns, poison gasses and the crushing weight of the ash and rock. Add to this the confusion that comes with such an event. Others survived by walking across the layers of hot rock and ash that was two meters thick in places. Later, when ordered to avoid the city by the emperor, people stayed out, except for those that would plunder the ruins. 40 years after the eruption Emperor Hadrian ordered the roads to be reopened and people began to repopulate the area. Today, castings of those who died when buried by volcanic ash are preserved in various locations throughout the city.

There have been many days of hopelessness for humankind throughout its history. Times when even the gods themselves would not lend a helping hand. Consequently just about every religion has tragic stories of disaster woven into its sacred texts. Flip through the pages of the Old Testament and you will find God's angry wrath against humans knitted into stories that had their roots in real natural disasters, some of which were obviously embellished for dramatic effect. It is rather obvious that the story tellers who created each tale searched for meaning and purpose in the face of each tragic event that unfolded. It is also just as obvious that story tellers tried to ascertain the true nature of god as they interpreted the events. Stories where God was wrathful, and vengeful and jealous became popular and were eventually canonized. While considering theological concepts like benevolence and justice, ancient philosophers struggled to explain the vast devastation.

False Hope

False hope occurs when we accept an untruth or paint a future for ourselves based on fantasy or self delusion. A psychological phenomenon called the "just world fallacy' or "just world phenomenon" is described as the tendency for people to believe, or want to believe that the world is a 'just' place. In some cases a person wants to believe it so badly that when tragedy occurs they look for reasons why those who suffered "must" have deserved their punishment. When deep faith dictates that God is *just* and *benevolent* it follows that any particular natural disaster must have been *justifiable to God* and was therefore necessary. Biblical authors must have wondered, "What did they do wrong to deserve that flood?" It is from these stories that the tenets of modern religion have blossomed. It comes as no surprise that some modern day evangelical preachers claimed that hurricane Katrina was the result of Gods dissatisfaction with New Orleans.

In an interview with Pastor John Hagee, Dennis Prager a right wing radio personality asked, "No, I'm only trying to understand that in the case of New Orleans, you do feel that God's hand was in it because of a sinful city? Hagee responded, "That it was a city that was planning a sinful conduct, yes."

If we apply this thought process and analyze Old Testament scripture, we can see that the story tellers who created those texts regularly explained natural disasters by use of this fallacious thinking. Biblical authors believed that the cities of Sodom and Gomorrah 'deserved what they got' due to impenitent sin (and homosexuality). They believed that those who died in the great flood (Noah's flood) deserved what they got because of their unrighteousness and that Egyptian people starved from drought because they worshipped false gods.

From this thinking it follows that to avoid disaster, disease or loss of income, one must be righteous. Consequently false hope is placed in the religious observance of ritual, reading of scripture and prayer.

Today, many fundamentalist Christians *study biblical prophesies* and seek confirmation of the bibles divine construction in modern day events. (See *http://www.100prophecies.org/page9.htm*)

They look for apocalyptic signs, thinking that they will soon be raptured. Sadly they ignore the misses, the many times when prophecy fails and they concentrate only on the hits, the events that fit the 'not so narrow' definitions commonly used by prophetic authors.

An interesting *study* shows that a large number of Americans (57.4%) actually believe that God can revive a dying patient. What is most shocking about this is that many of them demand that doctors continue with futile treatments that don't do any good for the patient who is terminal.

Can we blame people for not "getting it" when the time comes to face the death of a loved one? If one of my children were seriously injured I certainly would be prone to hope against all odds that they would pull through even though I am not a believer in the supernatural. It is quite normal for humans to resist change and to question those who tell us something contrary to what we want to hear.

This leaves doctors in a tough position, having to deal with families that just don't want to accept that their children, spouses or parents are going to die.

And all is not equal in the realm of belief; some of us have a lot further to go to accept a change such as the inevitable death of a loved one. Those who have been taught that God can heal the sick or raise the dead are "set up" to react differently than the rest of us, in my opinion. They are taught to expect a miracle and when a doctor tells them that this is not their day for a miracle the have a harder time in some respects with acceptance of the event. As a priest I was asked to perform healing prayers for people in a terminal condition, something which I was always hesitant to do. I explained my hesitancy by saying, "What we want here is that God's will be done, he may want to call you home."

As a result many are forced to revise their faith to allow for a God that does not perform miracles even when "two or more agree" which sets them at odds with their church community.

Matt 18:19,20 "Again, I tell you that if two of you on earth agree about anything you ask for, it will be done for you by my Father in heaven. For where two or three come together in my name, there am I with them."

I know, I talked to a number of people after the deaths of loved ones. One friend of mine talked about how the loss of his wife made him question if there really is a benevolent God and the result was his loss of faith, and eventually he suffered a loss of support from the church community he had grown up in. Another friend said that her idea of God changed as a result and now did not include a God that intervenes in the world's affairs, only a minor modification to her beliefs. It's too bad it set her at odds with those in her community.

From my experience in dealing with mourning people, these are very heavy issues to have to deal with when mourning the loss of a loved one. It is for this reason that I do not believe that the delusion of a loving or benevolent "intervening" God helps at all. I do believe that it would be better if we would face the reality that whether we are Christian, Muslim, Agnostic or Atheist, the mortality rate is 100 percent. The question of the existence of a creator and an afterlife is quite separate from belief in "miracles".

To some this issue is viewed as a cruel hoax perpetrated on the faithful by mainstream churches, and to others it is seen as open-mindedness at its best.

Why should open-mindedness hurt so badly, when reality works just fine? The answer is that people want hope, even if it's not real.

Real hope—it's hidden in the silver lining and our challenge is to find it

Today a scientific understanding of how the world functions has become popularized to the point where large weather and seismic systems can predict many of the worst natural disasters. We can move people out of the way long before tragedy occurs. In many countries geologists monitor active volcanoes and nearby communities are placed on alert whenever it's necessary. Disaster evacuation routes are planned based on weather patterns used to predict the extent of the affected area.

Scientists and civil engineers predicted the flooding of New Orleans prior to 2005, stating that if just one levee were to fail a large area within the city would be inundated with water. Stories about this flood potential were published in magazines and periodicals and were known to many politicians and the public long before the flood occurred. National Geographic, Scientific American and other magazines gave detailed explanations about how the levee system would fail. The politicians who knew about the reports did not recognize or understand the horrific consequences of the predictions, nor did they recognize the odds that a hurricane like Katrina could hit so precisely in the wrong area. As quickly as Katrina's weather patterns emerged the National Weather Service did their part and the government initiated an evacuation of over 90 percent of the residents of south east Louisiana. Katrina hit with catastrophic power, more than 50 levee breaches occurred and large areas within the city were flooded. The water was fifteen feet deep in some areas.

The folks who were left behind during the flood were mostly poor and elderly and the death toll reached 1,464. Some died due to drowning, others due to dehydration and yet others from natural causes exacerbated by a lack of medical attention due to the flooding. It is estimated that 135 are still missing.

Should we declare the New Orleans story a success on behalf of science or do we declare it a failure?

In reality science had done its part very well, the death toll would have been exponentially higher had it not been for the good forecasting and planning process that enabled the evacuation of ninety percent of the population. In my opinion, what failed was the political process; politicians did not heed the warnings issued by scientists about the failure of the levees. Where was their plan to evacuate the poor and elderly?

I suppose that the only good thing to come out of this tragedy was that it so clearly pointed out the relationship that should exist between science and government. It is a tragedy that people had to die for us to understand this. We ignore science at our peril.

What would the result have been if politicians *had* listened? There is a lesson to be learned here and the death toll and evacuation stories from Hurricane Gustav tell it rather well. The death toll from Gustav in the United States was 25. It appears that in the case of New Orleans, politicians have learned not to ignore science.

Humanism and Hope (My Own Spe Salvi)

Hope has been my salvation, hope has set me free. Hope comes from knowing that I *can* succeed. Hope comes from knowing that our loved ones have a future. The Humanist philosophy advocates using rational and scientific approaches to address the wide range of issues important to mankind.

Humanism is *how* we find hope.

Most people want to make their world a better place to live. We don't hesitate to use technology to make tasks simpler, to feed ourselves, to improve healthcare or to accomplish the mundane. We are a frail species subject to disease. Our use of the scientific method in testing medicines or developing technologies has greatly extended our average life span and lowered the child mortality rates in western countries. Smallpox is estimated to have killed 300-500 million people during the twentieth century and has now been eradicated due to world wide vaccinations. I cannot even begin to list all of the diseases that are now treatable or even curable all thanks to modern science. We did this for ourselves, humans taking care of humans.

Our minds are also frail and our ability to "know" is flawed. Our use of scientific skepticism has greatly helped us to determine the truth about how our world really works and to determine what we need to do to survive and prosper as a species. By using scientific skepticism we can make better decisions, we can tell good ideas from bad ones, we can tell which truths are simply made up and which ones are reproducible. Without scientific skepticism we could not have traveled to the moon or developed the germ theory of disease transmission. We did this for ourselves, humans helping humans.

Many western governments have extensive policies regarding humanitarian aid and they employ aid agencies to send food around the world in a matter of days or weeks. They literally send hope to those who have survived flooding or earthquakes. Cooperative efforts to feed millions of victims of war also occur through the United Nations.

The greatest achievements ever made by mankind came to light in cultures where free speech was encouraged. Where people were free to think and free to be rational and creative. Once we are set free, we can talk openly about what we do or don't believe. We can find healing, hope and freedom.

Unabated scientific enquiry has resulted in a means of enlightenment that needs to be nurtured and cared for. This enlightenment needs to be defended and evangelized to every corner of the earth. Countries that have embraced and defended equality and higher learning have reaped the benefits or prosperity and hope for their people. Where the humanistic principles of democracy, freedom, equality and peace go, prosperity and hope have a chance to follow.

Shortly before leaving the clergy, I struggled with how I could make the switch from a life of faith to the life I live today. I found a wonderful counselor who would take the time to listen, ask questions and challenge me. Leaving the church was one of the hardest things I have ever done even though I had actually left faith quite a while before. My lack of faith was the dirty little secret I had carried with me to many church meetings.

Without any judgment and with simple kindness he walked with me as I worked out the complicated issues of self doubt. I was especially fearful that some of the people in the congregation would get nasty (some did) and found that my counselor was there for me when times were rough. By being kind, lending a helping 'hand up' and by showing empathy, my counselor gave me hope. What's more, the hope extended to me was real, tangible and practical. It meant the world to me.

As we spoke about what I was contemplating my counselor asked why it was so important for me to leave. Why couldn't I just stay in church and not believe? My answer surprised me a bit, because I had never actually said it out loud before. "There are no longer any answers for me there, I just don't believe in God anymore. Besides, I am clergy and there is an expectation of faith". He accepted my answer and we moved on. That's all there was to it!

The freedom I found in his office did not exist in the church. At St. Aidan's there was no equality to be found for an agnostic or atheistic priest. I had tried to talk to my Bishop and other clergy who were friends but realized that they could not hear me. Their minds were clouded by their own need to restore my faith rather than let me be who I am.

The greatest lesson I have ever learned came from my counselor; real hope comes almost automatically when we find acceptance, equality, freedom to think, freedom to question and abundant human kindness. Every time *you* help someone *you* give them greater hope than any 'god' ever could.

The Humanist Association of Canada describes Humanism like this:

Humanism is a dynamic and religion-free way of life that affirms our ability and responsibility to lead ethical and meaningful lives, aspiring to the greater good of humanity. Humanism is guided by reason and scientific inquiry, inspired by music and art, and motivated by ethics, compassion and fairness.

The earliest written record of Humanist philosophy originated in ancient Greece thousands of years ago. This philosophy turned to human beings rather than gods to solve human problems. Democritus (460-351 BCE), a progressive thinker, atomic theorist, and Greek philosopher, asserted that human beings can set higher standards of personal integrity and social responsibility by guiding their lives by rational, moral, fair and compassionate means, rather than invoking imaginary or mystical sanctions.

Humanists support secular and scientific approaches to addressing the wide range of issues important to us all. This is why Humanists advocate keeping government and religion separate. Secular laws are the fairest and most realistic way that people of all faiths and philosophies can be considered as truly equal under the law.

Twelve Principles of Humanism

1. Humanism aims at the full development of every human being.
2. Humanists uphold the broadest application of democratic principles in all human relationships.
3. Humanists advocate the use of the scientific method, both as a guide to distinguish fact from fiction and to help develop beneficial and creative uses of science and technology.
4. Humanists affirm the dignity of every person and the right of the individual to maximum possible freedom compatible with the rights of others.
5. Humanists acknowledge human interdependence, the need for mutual respect and the kinship of all humanity.
6. Humanists call for the continued improvement of society so that no one may be deprived of the basic necessities of life, and for institutions and conditions to provide every person with opportunities for developing their full potential.
7. Humanists support the development and extension of fundamental human freedoms, as expressed in the United Nations Universal Declaration of Human Rights and supplemented by UN International Covenants comprising the United Nations Bill of Human Rights.
8. Humanists advocate peaceful resolution of conflicts between individuals, groups, and nations.
9. The humanist ethic encourages development of the positive potentialities in human nature, and approves conduct based on a sense of responsibility to oneself and to all other persons.
10. Humanists reject beliefs held in absence of verifiable evidence, such as beliefs based solely on dogma, revelation, mysticism or appeals to the supernatural.
11. Humanists affirm that individual and social problems can only be resolved by means of human reason, intelligent effort, critical thinking joined with compassion and a spirit of empathy for all living beings.
12. Humanists affirm that human beings are completely a part of nature, and that our survival is dependent upon a healthy planet that provides us and all other forms of life with a life-supporting environment.

Appendix 1

Further explanation of the concept "taught not to question"

In religion there are some basic ideas or 'memes' that draw people into a system of belief and retain them. These belief system mechanisms are universal to most religions but not all. All three of the memes that I am about to discuss are presented as systematic theologies, with variations depending on which religion or sect you encounter. (I have presented them as generalizations and have not backed them up with all of the well known scriptures from each religion. For a robust definition of the term 'meme' see *http://en.wikipedia.org/wiki/Meme*)

The three ideas and their mechanisms I am discussing are as follows:

1. Heaven and Hell, the creation of a situational disparity causing a sense of lost status, followed by a chance to regain the lost status via a form of salvation.
2. Without faith, it is impossible to please God.
3. You shall not test God.

1. *Creation of a situational disparity or incongruity, causing a sense of lost status, followed by a chance to regain the lost status via salvation. (Heaven and Hell)*

"For God so loved the world that he gave his one and only Son, that whoever believes in him shall not perish but have eternal life."
John 3:16 (NIV)

Read the words aloud slowly, "whoever believes in him shall not perish but have eternal life"

Christians are told that God first created mankind in an innocent or sinless state. Because of the sins of Eve, humans are now born into "sinful nature" and live in a fallen world. This innate sinful nature prevents them from spending their eternal lives in heaven and they are threatened with eternal fiery damnation. Either you are going to heaven or you are going to hell. Most sects of Christianity and Judaism maintain this "either-or" scenario in one form or another.

This idea, or meme, uses two concepts to create a sense of incongruity. First it tells you that we were created as eternal beings, which is completely untestable and without any foundation in science. Secondly, the concept of original sin creates a feeling of disparity that draws people to seek out a means to attain the eternal life in heaven that they have lost because of original sin. This meme has copied itself from it's original form in Judaism to virtually every sect of Christianity.

In its original form Judaism relied on animal sacrifice and a series complicated religious rituals to find forgiveness and a connection to God. For Christians, Jesus died on the cross as their perfect human sacrifice and is the propitiation for their sins, once and for all. A further relationship with God is maintained through the concept of prayer directly to God via the Holy Spirit, which is another meme all together.

In Islam all are considered to have been born pure, but have later sinned according to the law, and therefore need to repent and change their behaviour. Muslims generally believe that they work out their salvation through the guidance of Allah. Allah's mercy will allow them into heaven or his judgment will condemn them to hell.

Indoctrination usually occurs during childhood where statements of faith are presented as facts rather than philosophies. In almost every religious sect a ritual occurs with each child in order to mark them as belonging to the system of belief.

A similar disparity mechanism occurs in militant religious groups. Regardless of the particular religion, they are taught, for example, that "God promised you this particular holy land and 'they' have taken it from you, and are occupying it".

For some religious sects it is considered a virtue to die as a martyr in the struggle to regain God's will for the land. Families are greatly rewarded by the faith community when one of their children martyrs them self by a suicide attack. The "eternal" reward is assumed to be great for such an act of faith, which leads me to point two.

2. *"Without faith, it is impossible to please God" Hebrews 11:6 (NIV)*

The definition of faith is to believe something without evidence. "I accept this on faith", or "faith is a virtue" are statements commonly heard in virtually every religious experience.

This 'blind faith' mechanism strives to ensure that those who cannot verify why something is true will still accept it as truth. Adherents are intended to believe something and act as if they believe it with out understanding the logic or truthfulness of the assumptions that make up its components. You are not encouraged to look any further, just hold your nose and swallow.

I feel compelled to point out how important this function is in maintaining a system of religious adherence. People are literally taught not to think about things they cannot quite comprehend. To become more virtuous, you strengthen your faith and become better at believing. A person with the strongest faith accepts the reality of God, and often, the word of God, without questioning the validity of the concepts presented therein. What a virtue!

3. *You shall not test the Lord your God.*

> "You shall not put the LORD your God to the test, as you tested him at Massah.
>
> Exodus 17: 6-8 (NIV),

See also, Deuteronomy 6:14-16, Deut 9: 21-23, Deut 33: 7-9, Psalm 95:7-9, Matthew 4:6-8, Luke 4: 11-13.

The function of this mechanism is to extinguish any further attempts to question the viability of the belief system, or meme, by threatening the adherent with an angry God. It should be noted that in this otherwise unbelievable scenario the people encamped at Massah were desperate for water, their cattle were dieing and they openly questioned whether or not God was really leading them. There is no real scriptural argument against the case I make here as reference to the particular verse shows up quoted in five different places in the Old Testament, and twice in the New Testament. Christians and Jews are clearly discouraged from questioning God benevolence.

The message is clear, even when you are desperate and times are hard you should not question if there is a God.

These three memes: situational disparity, faith as a virtue and do not test, have brought many to their knees. They work together to stifle free thinking, encourage authoritarian rule and to ensure that those who do choose to raise questions are afraid of the consequences of free thought. It is important to remember that they are coupled with a host of other scriptures that refer to the consequences of disobeying God. Once a person had made the initial steps towards faith (and really believes that the particular God has executive power in this world) they are faced with eternal damnation should they consider leaving that particular faith.

Who is the devil now? What happened to free will?

Appendix 2

The problem with inerrant holy books

While some people claim to know what God is thinking, most of us do not hold to such a pretension. However, there is no shortage of people willing to follow those who claim such divine knowledge. Even today, religious leaders hold some form of sway over most of the population.

Many conservative Christians accept the Bible as the inerrant "Word of God" as a matter of faith, even though they have not fully read it. If you accept "biblical truths" as coming from God without any thought to question the basis of those beliefs you fall into this category and can be called a conservative Christian.

Many of the "truths" expressed in the bible are simply incorrect when held up to the light of modern science. I freely admit that many of the errors expressed in the bible are not necessarily moral in nature even though many are. Just the same, what do we make of the non-moral errors? The sun does not orbit the earth, although it is easy to see how theologians from the days of old came to this conclusion. In my opinion, the most important of these scriptural references to a geocentric cosmological system was Joshua 10:

"12 On the day the LORD gave the Amorites over to Israel, Joshua said to the LORD in the presence of Israel: "O sun, stand still over Gibeon, O moon, over the Valley of Aijalon." 13 So the sun stood still, and the moon stopped, till the nation avenged itself on its enemies, as it is written in the Book of Jashar. The sun stopped in the middle of the sky and delayed going down about a full day. Joshua 10:12-13 (NIV)

Were you to take these verses literally, as medieval theologians did, you might take them to be clear biblical evidence that indeed the Sun was moving, not the earth. Additional biblical proof for a moving Sun is seen in Ecclesiastes 1:5, where it is said: "The sun rises and the sun sets, and hurries back to where it rises"

Other biblical verses were interpreted as scriptural evidence that the Earth is fixed and immovable: Psalm 93:1 "1 The LORD reigns, he is robed in majesty; the LORD is robed in majesty and is armed with strength. The world is firmly established; it cannot be moved"

Psalm 104:5 "5 He set the earth on its foundations; it can never be moved."

1 Chronicles 16:30 "30 Tremble before him, all the earth! The world is firmly established; it cannot be moved"

Why does it matter that the bible is wrong about certain scientific issues? How is it that a disagreement about scriptural accuracy can end up in a squabble over Gods sovereignty?

In 1793 Thomas Paine said it eloquently in his book, The Age of Reason.

> *"If the belief of [biblical] errors not morally bad did no mischief, it would make no part of the moral duty of man to oppose and remove them. There was no moral ill in believing the earth was flat like a trencher, any more than there was moral virtue in believing it was round like a globe; neither was there any moral ill in believing that the Creator made no other world than this, any more than there was moral virtue in believing that he made millions, and that the infinity of space is filled with worlds. But when a system of religion is made to grow out of a supposed system of creation that is not true, and to unite itself therewith in a manner almost inseparable therefrom, the case assumes an entirely different ground. It is then that errors, not morally bad, become fraught with the same mischiefs as if they were."*

In plain English, when a system of religion is made to grow out of a supposed system of creation that is not true, it becomes inseparable from it. It is then that any small error, which may not in itself be morally wrong, becomes a moral problem. When the real truth is discovered about creation the entire system of belief comes into question.

Because conservative Christian leaders accept the Bible as the inerrant word of God they feel justified in persecuting those who oppose it, even when verifiable evidence of a different structure to the universe is found. The same problem arises on issues where the Bible is wrong on moral grounds, such as when Christians lobby against stem cell research, the equality of women, the validity of homosexual relationships or the efficacy of condom usage in Aids ravaged African countries.

The Varieties of Scientific Experience, published posthumously by Carl Sagan, he asked a most important question: *"Why is there no commandment exhorting us to learn?"*

Why?

Appendix 3

Table: Quick Reference— Ways of knowing

Method of Gaining Knowledge	Summary	Pitfall/Solution
Tenacity	Stories that have been always accepted as true with no means of verification, superstition, gossip.	—Personal Bias —Acceptance of untruths —No way to verify information —Leads to erroneous and sometimes dangerous beliefs —If it is a habit to use this method leaves one open to manipulation *Solution* —Avoid use of this method except for small decisions
Authority	Relies on information or answers from an expert in a particular subject area.	—Personal Bias —Leaves one open to manipulation —Sometimes we can't tell if the person knows what they are talking about *Solution* —Seek answers from a public forum where experts are encouraged to debate ideas (i.e. professional association University, College,) —Become your own expert

Faith	A variation of the method of Authority that requires unquestioning trust in authority, text or idea	—Personal Bias —Is used to create a truth where there may not be one to start with —Encourages adherents to an idea not to think critically about it *Solution* —Avoid the use of faith for anything but small decisions
Rationalism	Seeks answers by the use of logical reasoning	—Personal Bias —If premise statements are inaccurate the output from a logical deduction may also be inaccurate *Solution* —Use verified facts wherever possible
Empiricism	Uses observation or direct sensory experience to obtain knowledge	—Experimenter bias —Hypothesis must produce testable predictions —Operational definitions must be clear and accurate to ensure validity of results —It is possible to carry forward unchecked bias or mistakes from earlier experiments. —Empiricism by definition is limited to the natural world

REFERENCES

1. Sagan, Carl. (2006), The Varieties of Scientific Experience, a personal view of the search for god. Edited by Ann Druyan, Penguin Group (Canada), Toronto Ontario, Canada M4P 2Y3
2. Paine, Thomas, (1793) The Age of Reason, edited by Moncure D. Conway. Available for free download at, *http://www.infidels.org/library/historical/ thomas_paine/age_of_reason/*
3. The Collects, Epistles, and Gospels from the 1549, 1552 and 1559 Books of Common Prayer *http://justus.anglican.org/resources/bcp/1549/ Readings_HolyWeek_1549.htm#Good%20Friday*
4. A Letter To My Curious Friends. Published March 2008, by Jeffrey Olsson, a former Priest in the Anglican Church of Canada. *http://www.members. shaw.ca/jdolsson/Friends.htm*
5. Gravetter Frederick J, Forzano Lori-Ann B (2006). Research Methods for the Behavioral Sciences, second edition (pages 4-22) Belmont, Ca: Wadsworth/Thomson Learning
6. Dawkins, R. (2006), The GOD Delusion, Houghton Mifflin Company, New York, New York 10003.
7. Diamond, Jared: *Guns, Germs, and Steel: The Fates of Human Societies.* W.W. Norton & Company, March 1997. *ISBN 0-393-03891-2*
8. Sagan, Carl, "*The Demon-Haunted World: Science As a Candle in the Dark*". *Ballantine Books,* March 1997 *ISBN 0-345-40946-9*
9. Attenborough, David, *Journeys To The Past*, David Attenborough Productions, Butler and Tanner Ltd, Frome and London, 1981, ISBN 0 7188-2507-1

10. Benedict XVI, Encyclical Letter SPE SALVI, of the Supreme Pontiff Benedict XVI to the Bishops Priests and Deacons Men and Women Religious and all the lay faithful on Christian Hope, Nov 30, 2007, from Vatican internet website. *http://www.vatican.va/holy_father/benedict_xvi/ encyclicals/documents/hf_ben-xvi_enc_20071130_spe-salvi_en.html*
11. Wooden, Cindy, Catholic News Service, Abortion is crime against society, says Pope Benedict Abortion is crime against society, says Pope Benedict, (Dec 5th 2005) *http://www.catholicnews.com/data/stories/cns/0506904.htm*
12. Of the Morals of the Catholic Church, St. Augustine of Hippo in A.D. 388, translated by the Rev. Richard Stothert, New Advent website: Copyright © 2008 by Kevin Knight. *http://www.newadvent.org/fathers/1401.htm*
13. Jackson. E, Subjective Study of Visual Aberrations, Trans Am Ophthalmol Soc. 1938; 36: 46-54 *http://www.pubmedcentral.nih.gov/pagerender.fcgi?artid=1315728&pageindex=1*
14. Adams, Douglas, 1998, Digital Biota 2 conference speech, Cambridge U.K, from the internet. *http://www.biota.org/people/douglasadams/*
15. Zygar, Mikhail, in Kommersant, Russia's Online Daily, Sept 26, 2007, *http://www.kommersant.com/page.asp?id=808259*
16. Kirby, Alex, in BBC News, International version, May 9, 2003, *http://news.bbc.co.uk/2/hi/science/nature/3014747.stm*
17. University of Chicago (2008, July 12). Children Are Naturally Prone To Be Empathic And Moral. *ScienceDaily*. Retrieved July 12, 2008, from *http://www.sciencedaily.com/releases/2008/07/080711080957.htm*
18. Decety et al. **Who caused the pain? An fMRI investigation of empathy and intentionality in children**. *Neuropsychologia*, 2008; DOI: *10.1016/j.neuropsychologia.2008.05.026*
19. Glines.C.V, The Cargo Cults, Air Force Magazine, The Journal of the Air Force, January 1991, Vol 74, No.1, *http://www.afa.org/magazine/1991/0191cargo.asp*
20. Raffaele, Paul, In John They Trust, Smithsonian Magazine, Smithsonian.com, Feb 2006. *http://www.smithsonianmag.com/people-places/john.html*
21. Letter 2808—Darwin, C. R. to Gray, Asa, 18 May [1860], Darwin Correspondence Project, Retrieved July 19th 2008, from *http://www.darwinproject.ac.uk/darwinletters/calendar/entry-2808.html*

22. Letter 2814—Darwin, C. R. to Gray, Asa, 22 May [1860], Darwin Correspondence Project, Retrieved July 19th 2008, from *http://www. darwinproject.ac.uk/darwinletters/calendar/entry-2814.html*
23. Ferry, James, In The Courts Of The Lord: A Gay Priest's Story, The Crossroad Publishing Company, Inc. (September 25, 1994)
24. Spitzer, Robert L, (December, 1973) Homosexuality: Proposed Change in DSM-H, The American Psychiatric Association. (Retrieved August 4, 2008) *www.psychiatryonline.com/DSMPDF/DSM-II_Homosexuality_ Revision.pdf*
25. Book of Common Prayer, THE PREFACE TO THE CANADIAN REVISION OF 1918 ALTERED IN 1959, Prayer book society of Canada website. Retrieved August 24th 2008. *http://prayerbook. ca/bcp/1959_preface.html*
26. Press Release, Anglican News Service (ANS), (1978, Feb 3), Retreived August 4, 2008 from *http://www2.anglican.ca/faith/hs/hsrh.htm*
27. The Montreal Declaration (June 1994), From Anglican Essentials website, Retrieved August 24th, 2008. *http://www.anglicanessentials. ca/pdf/montreal_declaration_aec.pdf*
28. Sison, Marites, N, Anglican Journal (October 1, 2006), Archbishop disciplined for performing same sex marriage, (Retrieved August 4 2008) *http://www.anglicanjournal.com/100/article/archbishop-disciplined-for-performing-same-sex-marriage/*
29. Sison, Marites, N, Anglican Journal (October 1, 2004), Church awaits critical commission report, (Retrieved August 4, 2008) *http://www. anglicanjournal.com/issues/2004/130/oct/08/article/church-awaits-critical-commission-report/*
30. Anglican Journal, (Dec 1 2007), Montreal Synod Votes Yes to Blessings, Retrieved August 4 2008, *http://www.anglicanjournal.com/issues/2007/133/ dec/10/article/montreal-synod-votes-yes-to-blessings/*
31. Sison, Marites, N, Anglican Journal, (Oct 13 2007), Ottawa Votes Yes to Same Sex Blessings, Retrieved August 4 2008, *http://www.anglicanjournal. com/sexuality-debate/055/article/ottawa-votes-yes-to-same-sex-blessings/*
32. De Santis, Solange, Anglican Journal, (May 27, 2008), Huron Says Yes to Same Sex Blessings, Retrieved August 4 2008, *http://www.anglicanjournal. com/sexuality-debate/055/article/huron-says-yes-to-same-sex-blessings-1/*

33. Sison, Marites, N, Anglican Journal, (August 3, 2007) Bishops end conference with 'wide agreement' on moratoria for same-sex blessings, cross-border interventions, and ordination of gay bishops, says Williams, Retrieved August 4th 2008, http://www.anglicanjournal.com/sexuality-debate/055/article/bishops-end-conference-with-wide-agreement-on-moratoria-for-same-sex-blessings-cross-border-inter/
34. Goudarzi, Sara, MSNBC, (Nov 16, 2006) Gay animals out of the closet? First-ever museum display shows 51 species exhibiting homosexuality, (Retrieved August 4, 2008) http://www.msnbc.msn.com/id/15750604/
35. Bidstrup, Scott (no date), The Natural "Crime Against Nature" A Brief Survey of Homosexual Behaviors In Animals, (Retrieved August 4, 2008) http://www.bidstrup.com/sodomy.htm
36. Coghlan, Andy, New Scientist (16 June, 2008) Gay brains structured like those of the opposite sex, (Retrieved August 4, 2008) http://www.newscientist.com/article/dn14146-gay-brains-structured-like-those-of-the-opposite-sex.html
37. Hall, Joseph, Toronto Star, (June 17, 2008), Gayness linked to brain, (Retrieved August 4, 2008) http://www.thestar.com/article/444461
38. Savik, Ivanka and Lindstrom, Per, (April 30,2008) PET and MRI show differences in cerebral asymmetry and functional connectivity between homo- and heterosexual subjects, (Retrieved, August 4, 2008) http://www.pnas.org/content/early/2008/06/13/0801566105.abstract
39. BBC News, (June 27, 2006), Womb environment 'makes men gay, (Retrieved August 4 2008) http://news.bbc.co.uk/2/hi/health/5120004.stm
40. Martin, Bruce, (2006, Aug 24) Calvary Temple—Doubt, (Retreived August 4, 2008), http://www.ctwinnipeg.com/radio-and-tv.aspx
41. Mills, David, Atheist Universe, (2004) edited by Lily Chou, Ulysses Press, Berkely CA. www.ulyssespress.com
42. Curry, Bill and Howlette, Karen,(April 24 2007) Natives died in droves as Ottawa ignored warnings, retreived Sept 19th 2008, http://www.globeadvisor.com/servlet/ArticleNews/story/gam/20070424/SCHOOLS24
43. CBC News, (April 28th 2008), A timeline of residential schools, retrieved sept 19, 2008, http://www.cbc.ca/canada/story/2008/05/16/f-timeline-residential-schools.html

44. CBC News, (November 23 2005), School abuse victims getting $1.9B, retrieved sept 19, 2008, *http://www.cbc.ca/story/canada/national/2005/11/23/residential-package051123.html*
45. RCMP Fact Sheets, (25/09/2007), Indian Residential Schools, retreived sept 19 2008, *http://www.rcmp-grc.gc.ca/factsheets/fact_irs_e.htm*
46. Coneely, Sean, Informity News, Canada Apologizes, Compensates Native People, retreived Sept 19, 2008, *http://www.informify.com/top-stories/47-law-civil-rights/222-canada-apologizes-compensates-native-people*
47. Prager, Dennis, Interview with John Nagee, retreived Sept 19, 2008, *http://thinkprogress.org/2008/04/23/hagee-katrina-mccain/*
49. *http://www.100prophecies.org/page9.htm* (A web page exemplifying the study of Biblical Prophesy)
50. Views of the Public and Trauma Professionals on Death and Dying From Injuries, Lenworth M. Jacobs, MD, MPH; Karyl Burns, RN, PhD; Barbara Bennett Jacobs Arch Surg. 2008;143(8):730-735. *http://archsurg.ama-assn.org/cgi/content/abstract/143/8/730*
51. Louisiana Department of Health and Hospitals study of Hurricane Katrina *http://www.dhh.louisiana.gov/offices/page.asp?ID=192&Detail=5248*
52. Acheivements of the United Nations, *http://www.un.org/aboutun/achieve.htm*

Wikipedia Links cited in this document: Please note that I have always used original sources for each point that I have made, however I feel that the addition of Wikipedia links provides a rich source of complimentary information that otherwise may not be available to an "online" reader.—jo

1. Meme. (2006, December 29). In Wikipedia, The Free Encyclopedia. Retrieved 22:33, January 1, 2007, from *http://en.wikipedia.org/w/index.php?title=Meme&oldid=97196926*
2. Canadian residential school system. (2008, April 17). In Wikipedia, The Free Encyclopedia. Retrieved 17:35, April 21, 2008, from *http://en.wikipedia.org/w/index.php?title=Canadian_residential_school_system&oldid=206137352*
3. Cargo cult. (2008, May 13). In Wikipedia, The Free Encyclopedia. Retrieved 17:38, May 23, 2008, from *http://en.wikipedia.org/w/index.php?title=Cargo_cult&oldid=212124437*

4. John Frum. (2008, May 10). In *Wikipedia, The Free Encyclopedia*. Retrieved 14:08, May 24, 2008, from *http://en.wikipedia.org/w/index.php?title=John_Frum&oldid=211453819*
5. Karen Armstrong. (2008, April 30). In *Wikipedia, The Free Encyclopedia*. Retrieved 19:14, May 6, 2008, from *http://en.wikipedia.org/w/index.php?title=Karen_Armstrong&oldid=209339943*

References for Quotations

Unless otherwise stated, All scriptures quoted in this document are taken from the HOLY BIBLE, NEW INTERNATIONAL VERSION. Copyright 1973, 1978, 1984 international Bible Society. Used by permission of Zondervan Bible Publishers.